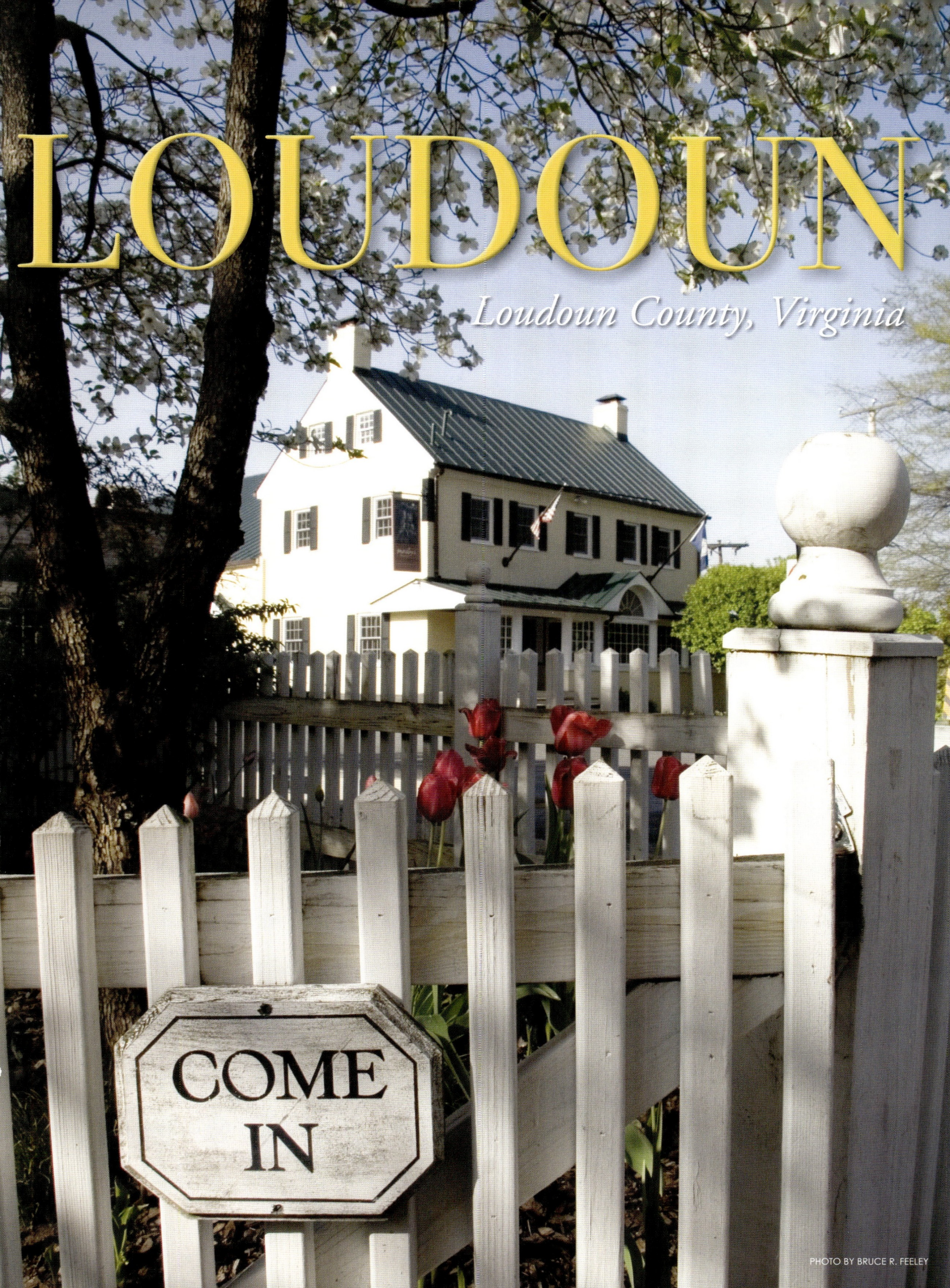

LOUDOUN

Loudoun County, Virginia

COME IN

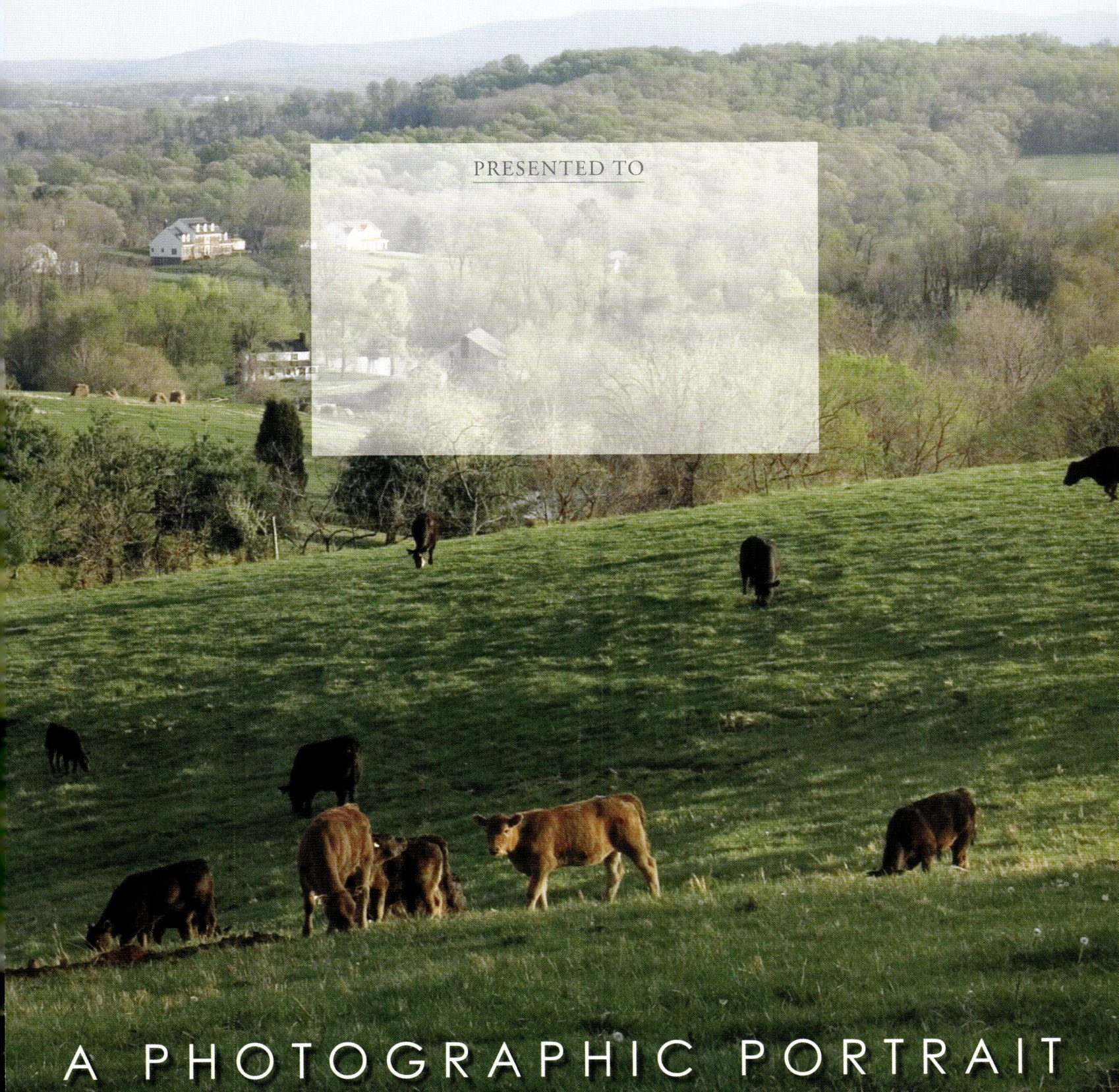

LOUDOUN

Loudoun County, Virginia

PRESENTED TO

A PHOTOGRAPHIC PORTRAIT

LOUDOUN

Loudoun County, Virginia

A PHOTOGRAPHIC PORTRAIT

EDITOR . . . . Rob Levin
PUBLISHER . . . . Barry Levin
ASSOCIATE PUBLISHER . . . . Bob Sadoski
COMMUNITY LIAISON . . . . Lorna Clarke
SENIOR EDITOR . . . . Renée Peyton
ASSOCIATE EDITOR . . . . Rena Distasio
PROJECT DIRECTOR . . . . Cheryl Sadler
PHOTO EDITOR . . . . Jill Dible
PROJECT COORDINATOR . . . . Muriel Diguette
WRITERS . . . . Kimberly DeMeza, Rena Distasio,
    Grace Hawthorne, Amy Meadows, Regina Roths
COPY EDITOR . . . . Bob Land
BOOK DESIGN . . . . Jill Dible
JACKET DESIGN . . . . Kevin Smith
PREPRESS . . . . Vickie Berdanis
PHOTOGRAPHERS . . . . . Jeanette Burkle, Thomas S. England,
    Bruce Feeley, Dave Galen, Scott Indermaur, Alan S. Weiner

RIVERBEND BOOKS
A division of Bookhouse Group, Inc.
Creating images your community will show the world.

Published by Riverbend Books
an Imprint of Bookhouse Group, Inc.
818 Marietta Street, NW
Atlanta, Georgia 30318
www.riverbendbooks.net
404.885.9515

ISBN: 978-1-883987-29-9

Library of Congress Cataloging-in-Publication Data

Loudoun, Loudoun County, Virginia : a photographic portrait / [editor, Rob Levin].
   p. cm.
ISBN 978-1-883987-29-9 (alk. paper)
1. Loudoun County (Va.)–History. 2. Loudoun County (Va.)–Pictorial works. 3. Loudoun County (Va.)–Social life and customs. 4. Loudoun County (Va.)–Economic conditions. 5. Business enterprises–Virginia–Loudoun County. I. Levin, Rob, 1955-
  F232.L8L69 2007
  975.5'28–dc22
                    2006039659

Whatever your idea of fun, it's a good bet you'll find it in Loudoun County. Whether it's burlap bag races at the Delaplane Strawberry Festival, an outdoor concert in a park, a museum exhibit, or a sports event, the area is brimming with things to do and see for the whole family.

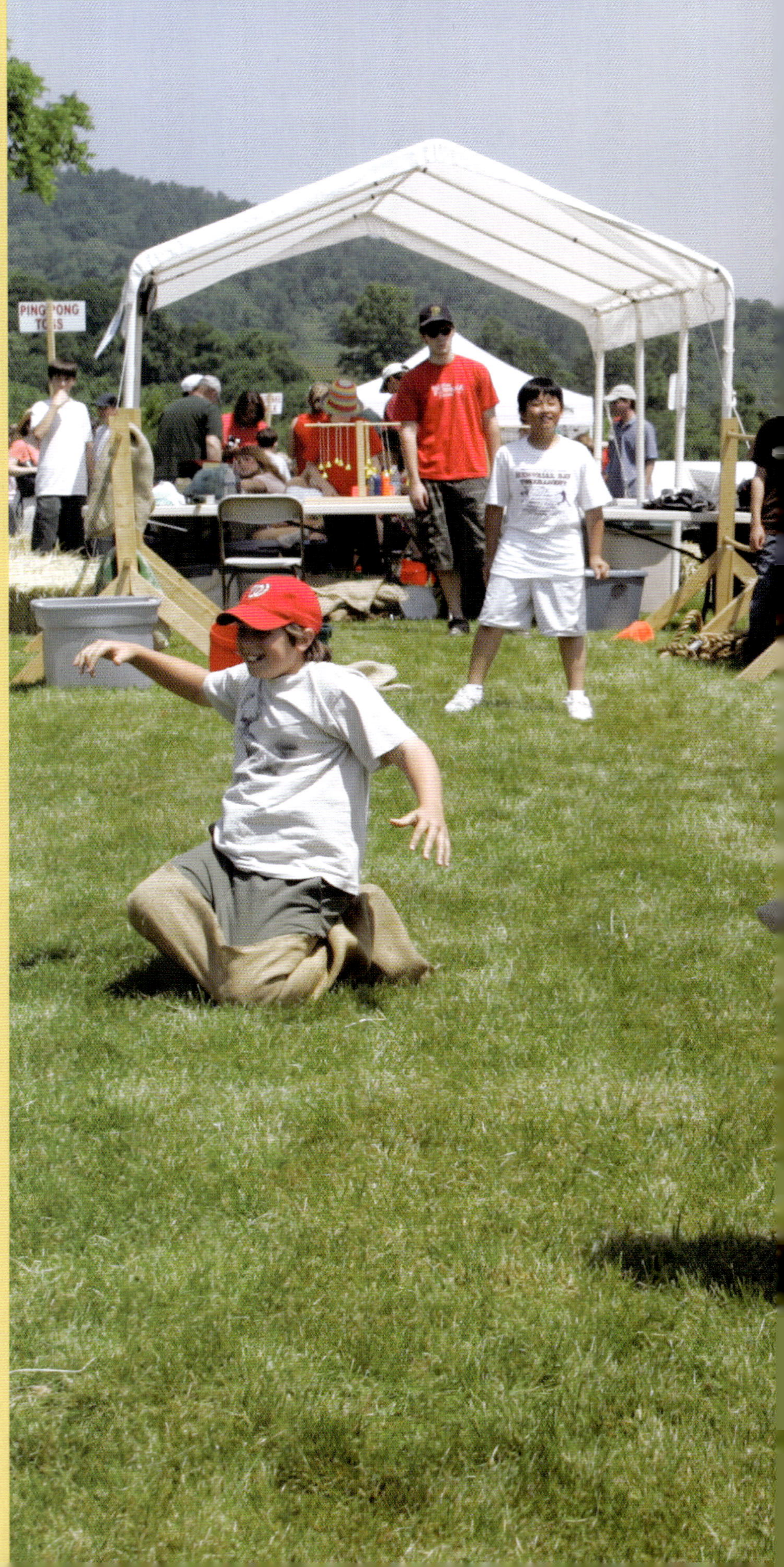

Statistics can tell you certain things about Loudoun County—for instance, that it's currently the fastest-growing county in the United States, as well as its richest. But what the numbers can't tell you is how great it is to live here, in a perfect balance between urban and rural, historic and modern, enterprise and leisure. And they certainly can't tell you about the people: the 255,000-plus individuals who don't just make up a population, but the area's character—hospitable, hardworking, and family-friendly.

Contents

LOUDOUN

Loudoun County, Virginia

A PHOTOGRAPHIC PORTRAIT

WOULD NOT HAVE BEEN POSSIBLE WITHOUT THE SUPPORT OF THE FOLLOWING SPONSORS:

American Home Mortgage • AOL • Dulles Area Association of REALTORS®, Inc. • F & M Title & Escrow • George Mason University • HCA Virginia Holiday Inn at Carradoc Hall • Howard Hughes Medical Institute • Inova Loudoun Hospital • Lansdowne Resort • Loudoun County • Loudoun Medical Group M.C. Dean • Mercantile Potomac Bank • Moore Cadillac Hummer • National Electronic Warranty • Nova Medical Group & Urgent Care Center, Inc. RE/MAX Leaders, Sherry Wilson & Co. • The Ritz-Carlton Golf Club, Creighton Farms • The Town of Leesburg • United Airlines

Foreword

Welcome to Loudoun County! As one of America's most prosperous and fastest-growing counties, Loudoun is a special place where the dynamic, cutting-edge promise of technology and science meet the charm of its abundant Colonial- and Civil War-era history.

Within Loudoun County is some of America's most beautiful pastoral scenery, not far from the nation's most advanced research in bioscience at the Howard Hughes Medical Institute. Located just a forty-five-minute drive from the monuments and the halls of power of the nation's capital, Loudoun County typifies America's promise to the world as the land of opportunity.

Those opportunities—from the economic to the educational, from the historic to the cultural—abound in almost limitless supply. Whether your dream is to open an award-winning winery, achieve the next great scientific discovery, or simply pursue the career or business of your dreams, Loudoun is the place to do it.

Over the past ten years, the population of Loudoun County has nearly doubled as people have flocked to the burgeoning county, drawn by its unbeatable combination of a growing economy, quaint and historic towns, and bucolic rural landscapes.

In recent years, Loudoun's growth has defied national trends, fueled largely by a recession-proof economy powered by two massive engines—the U.S. federal government and Washington Dulles International Airport, located on the county's eastern edge.

Loudoun's unparalleled quality of life is its greatest asset. The view from a corporate campus can include mountain vistas, rolling hills, and country lanes, creeks, and rivers. Nearby are quaint, historic towns that draw visitors and residents alike. Loudoun's horse country has a timeless quality that few places can match.

Loudoun's peerless quality of life gives the county a strong edge when it is competing for businesses, jobs, and capital investment. As a result, the county has become a prominent business and technology center. Its business community includes world-renowned corporate headquarters such as that of America Online, and defense and technology leaders like Lockheed Martin, Computer Sciences Corporation, Orbital Sciences Corporation, and Telos Corporation.

Despite the presence of these corporate giants, most of Loudoun's companies are small businesses, with an increasing number of entrepreneurs starting their own businesses.

Like the county it serves, the Loudoun County Chamber of Commerce is a dynamic, fast-growing organization that offers cutting-edge programs and services with the hometown charm and openness that makes all of our members feel like they are part of something special. That is why the Loudoun Chamber is the largest business organization in the county and, with almost fourteen hundred members, the second-largest chamber of commerce in the entire Washington, D.C., area.

Most of those Chamber members are small businesses that take advantage of the organization's opportunities for networking and marketing goods and services. The Chamber's board is a Who's Who of community leaders, and those who want to become community leaders know that getting involved in the Chamber is virtually a prerequisite for moving up.

Whether you've lived here all your life or maybe never visited Loudoun before, the remarkable images captured in this book will take you to a place unlike many others in the world. Welcome to Loudoun County, where American history continues to be made.

Tony Howard
President
Loudoun County Chamber of Commerce

What better way to offset a hot summer day than with the perfect watermelon? Chase Speacht helps his dad, Charles, find just the right one—juicy, sweet, and bursting with goodness—at a local farmers market just outside Leesburg. Currently, the Loudoun Valley HomeGrown Markets Association sponsors seven farmers markets in Loudoun County. Each is designated as a HomeGrown, Producer Only Market, meaning that the sellers are also the growers. These markets can provide buyers the freshest produce available in the region, much of which is picked and brought to market within twenty-four hours.

Chapter One

LIVE!

No doubt Loudoun County's current ranking as one of the fastest-growing and most prosperous counties in the nation makes it an irresistible place to put down roots. But there's more to the story than just economics. A closer look reveals the secret to Loudoun's exceptional quality of life: its diversity.

Boasting a storied past that goes back to the early days of our nation's founding, Loudoun County was part of the original 5-million-acre land grant given by King Charles II of England to seven noblemen in 1649. Settlers began entering the region as early as 1720, and many of those towns are still booming today, attracting both visitors and permanent residents with their mix of historic charm and modern amenities.

County planners also work to ensure the region retains much of its historic rural character. Not only are numerous family farms, ranches, and horse farms still in existence, many new residential developments are committed to curbing sprawl and preserving open space. Loudoun is also home to a noted alternative residential community. Located north of

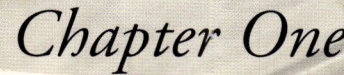

Leesburg, EcoVillage offers residents a safe, family-friendly community that emphasizes green building and careful management of the surrounding natural environment.

Whether residents choose to live in town or out, all enjoy quick access to Washington, D.C., and all the advantages offered by one of the most culturally and economically progressive cities in the nation. Thanks in large part to this proximity, Loudoun's economy is defined by numerous knowledge-based industries. To provide for those industries, the county's educational system has developed into one of the best in the nation, supporting a top-notch public school system as well as many colleges and universities. Many of these higher learning centers lie along Route 7's "Learning Corridor," and represent the highest concentration of postsecondary academic institutions in Virginia.

Whether setting up shop or starting a family, commuting to our nation's power center or retiring in bucolic bliss, Loudoun County residents enjoy one of the best, most diverse qualities of life in the nation.

Much of Loudoun County is still very much horse country. One of its oldest hunt clubs, the Loudoun County Hunt Club, established in 1894, still provides its members with opportunities to socialize and enjoy their sport. The club holds weekly trail rides and anywhere from fifty to seventy hunts per year from September to March. Its point-to-point races, in which riders compete to see who has the fastest horse for riding and jumping across country while on the hunt, is held each year in mid-April at Oatlands Plantation.

PHOTO BY THOMAS S. ENGLAND

Community Service . . . A Noble Mission

Helping those who help others

For nearly one hundred years, the Ladies Board of Inova Loudoun Hospital has demonstrated an inspiring commitment to supporting quality community health care. A nonprofit organization whose mission is to promote goodwill between the hospital and the community, the Ladies Board is devoted to raising funds for patient care, nursing scholarships, and hospital projects.

When Loudoun Hospital was established in Leesburg on June 5, 1912, its founders quickly realized that help would be needed with housekeeping and fund-raising. The women of the community answered the call, and a few weeks later the Ladies Board was born. Comprising forty volunteers representing Leesburg's churches and the surrounding communities, Ladies Board members literally rolled up their sleeves and took on the day-to-day operations of keeping the hospital running.

As a first order of duty, the Ladies Board organized an open house and invited the community to bring donations to support the hospital—everything from furniture to bedding to groceries, as well as financial contributions. As a result, for many years afterward the Ladies Board would maintain the hospital's equipment and provide supplies.

The same generous spirit that organized the hospital's first Donation Day manifests itself today in one of the Ladies Board's most successful fund-raisers, the Annual Hospital Rummage Sale. Established in 1938 and now held for two days in October, the sale has earned a reputation as the biggest treasure hunt and bargain-shopping extravaganza in the area, drawing local and out-of-state shoppers. It is also recognized as one of the Board's largest fund-raisers. In 2006, the event exceeded a record $120,000, thanks to this dedicated group of women.

All donation, all volunteer, all the time, the Twice Is Nice thrift shop is full of fun finds that run the gamut from clothing to housewares. Located at 305 East Market Street in Leesburg's Tollhouse Shopping Center and open 10 a.m. to 4 p.m. Monday through Saturday, Twice Is Nice is run entirely by volunteers, including two-year veteran Sandra Fulton (shown here).

In recent years, the Ladies Board has extended the concept of turning hard work and business savvy into highly successful retail operations. The volunteer-staffed gift shop at the hospital has contributed hundreds of thousands toward patient care. Since opening in 1990, the Twice Is Nice thrift shop, with its quality previously owned clothing, accessories, furniture, kitchen items, and books, is also doing its share to increase the board's million-dollar pledge to the hospital.

Both locations keep piggy banks on the counters for shoppers to drop in change for the hospital's nursery. Named after longtime member Polly Clemens, the fund's contributions include weight scales, nursing monitors, rocking chairs, and a baby swing.

The Ladies Board also continues its long-standing commitment to nursing. Annual Ladies Board Nursing Scholarships recognize and award dozens of qualifying nurses and students, supporting nursing professionals and those entering the field. The Lights of Love program, in which donors annually purchase a memorial light for the holiday trees at Inova Loudoun's Lansdowne and Cornwall campuses, offers the community a heartfelt way to honor and remember loved ones and friends.

Fueled by seemingly endless energy, creativity, and commitment, the Ladies Board helps ensure the continued availability of high-quality health care in Loudoun County. For generations of Loudoun women the organization has also become a way of life, the opportunity to participate in a legacy, and a proud tradition of personal and shared community service. ✦

The Ladies Board helps ensure the continued availability of high-quality health care in Loudoun County.

Gift shop committee member Teck Russell (left) and gift shop manager Sue Ulland discuss the placement of some new items. Open Monday through Saturday and staffed by Ladies Board members and volunteers, the gift shop provides customers with a wide selection of cards, boutique gifts, flowers, and small home décor items while raising funds for worthy hospital projects.

PHOTO BY THOMAS S. ENGLAND

For the school year 2005–2006, nearly four thousand boys and over three thousand girls participated in interscholastic sports at Loudoun County's ten high schools, which offer students over sixteen varsity sports. And it's not just about the boys. Loudoun County high schools support excellent girls' sports programs as well. Two of the district's talented teams include the Broad Run Spartans and the Stone Bridge Bulldogs, both located in Ashburn. The two schools have enjoyed a longtime friendly rivalry, especially in soccer and softball, two sports at which their girls' teams consistently excel. Stone Bridge held the State AA title for girls' soccer in 2005, and Broad Run took State in softball in 2000 and girls' soccer in 2001.

PHOTO BY BRUCE R. FEELEY

PHOTO BY BRUCE R. FEELEY

PHOTO BY BRUCE R. FEELEY

PHOTO BY BRUCE R. FEELEY

PHOTO BY BRUCE R. FEELEY

The Old Dominion University, Northern Virginia Center, is conveniently located on Route 7 in Sterling, adjacent to the Northern Virginia Community College Loudoun campus. In addition to providing students and working professionals with a physical presence for class participation, the state-of-the-art center brings access to ODU's comprehensive distance learning programs.

PHOTO BY BRUCE R. FEELEY

Education That Goes the Distance

Degrees for professional and adult students on-site and online

Old Dominion University, a Virginia public doctoral research institution located in historic Norfolk, Virginia, is a national leader in technology-mediated distance learning programs. Today, Old Dominion University's distance learning network consists of nearly fifty locations at community colleges, higher education centers, and military locations throughout Virginia and at sites in Arizona, Washington state, and the Bahamas, and on U.S. Navy ships deployed around the globe.

Through its Northern Virginia Center located in Sterling, Virginia, adult students and working professionals in Loudoun County have access to undergraduate and graduate degree programs in business, education, engineering technology, and health care, with two doctoral programs and several certificate programs also offered via distance learning.

With degree programs offered in a range of formats and schedules, combined with quality on-site and online student services, ODU makes it convenient for working professionals to pursue their academic goals in Loudoun County. In addition, ODU has fostered collaborative transfer articulation agreements with the Commonwealth of Virginia Community College System, to include the Northern Virginia Community College, Loudoun Campus located adjacent to the Center.

Old Dominion University is committed to a quality learning environment and employs experienced, qualified faculty, many of whom have earned distinguished awards for their academic research and teaching. And ODU maintains accreditation by the Commission on Colleges of the Southern Association of Colleges and Schools. ✦

ODU makes it convenient for working professionals to pursue their academic goals in Loudoun County.

PHOTO BY BRUCE R. FEELEY

The Academy of Science is a new Loudoun County public school where students take science, math, and research courses at the academy and all other subjects at their home school on the opposite days. This schedule enables students to maintain involvement in academic and extracurricular activities at their home school while participating in a challenging research-based math and science program. A student at the academy can expect to acquire the skills necessary to ask sophisticated scientific questions and conduct research. Top: Olivia DeMay carefully examines a culture of *Nasonia vitiripennis*, a parasitic wasp used at the academy in genetic studies. Right: Physics is fun when students investigate the relationship of kinetic and potential energy in a roller coaster designed from pipe insulation. Above: Bianca Garramore and Simrati Rahi add nutrient to a bacteria colony. One of the fastest-growing public school systems in the nation, Loudoun County Public Schools serves approximately fifty thousand students each year. The system's slogan, "a climate for success," is more than words: mean scores on the Scholastic Aptitude Test (SAT) surpass state and national averages by a significant margin.

PHOTO BY BRUCE R. FEELEY

PHOTO BY BRUCE R. FEELEY

There are myriad choices of where to live in Loudoun County. From any one of the seven historic towns and numerous villages that make up the area, or the newer subdivisions like Lansdowne, it's easy to feel a sense of place in Loudoun. Embraced by the mountains, in the middle of hunt and wine country, and at the crossroads of history and today, the area offers a near-perfect blend of the best of all worlds.

PHOTO BY BRUCE R. FEELEY

A Long-Standing Tradition

Their spirit goes beyond medicine

It is rare to find a hospital and a community as well matched as Inova Loudoun Hospital and Loudoun County, Virginia. Both take pride in their history, value the latest technology, have outstanding reputations, are growing, and provide excellent opportunities for employment, and both are spoken of highly by the people who live or work there.

The residents of Loudoun County have received quality care from Inova Loudoun Hospital since 1912. As a not-for-profit health-care institution, the hospital has no stockholders to satisfy, only the citizens who count on it to provide for their needs.

Everyone who enters the main entrance of the hospital is welcomed with sunlight streaming through large windows. There are comfortable, open common areas for family and friends.

Staff, physicians, nurses, and support personnel all seem to agree that Inova Loudoun Hospital is not only a great place to be a patient, it is a great place to work. It offers the latest technology used by people who care about each other and the people they serve.

For a more complete picture of what Inova Loudoun Hospital has to offer, take a closer look at a few specific areas. The first area is the Birthing Inn, where new life begins. Each of the nine private labor suites offers a homelike atmos-

PHOTO BY SCOTT INDERMAUR

Families will have a wonderful experience at the Birthing Inn.

PHOTO BY ALAN S. WEINER

phere with specialty lighting, soaking tubs, and tasteful furnishings plus the best medical equipment and personnel immediately available for mother and infant. The Family Education Series offers information and support to mothers and family members throughout pregnancy and after the new mother leaves the hospital.

Thanks to the leadership and generosity of the Schaufeld family, the Inova Heart and Vascular Institute opened the Schaufeld Family Heart Center at Inova Loudoun Hospital. This is the county's first and only cardiac catheterization lab. "Because we can now see a patient's coronary arteries in real time on a computer screen, we can map out the best treatment, be it medication, a coronary stent, or a bypass," said Dr. Robert Harron, an interventional cardiologist.

Another important area of Inova Loudoun Hospital is the Mary Elizabeth Miller Radiation Oncology Center. The center's state-of-the-art equipment includes a treatment planning system that enables physicians to localize treatment areas accurately. The center also provides education and support for patients and families in a warm, comforting environment. All the support groups/programs are free and open to the community.

The most recent addition to the hospital is the Pediatric Emergency Department. Because treating children is different from treating adults, this department is designed with child-sized equipment and is staffed with physicians specially trained in pediatric

The residents of Loudoun County have received quality care from Inova Loudoun Hospital since 1912.

Robert Felter, MD, loves coming to work every day at the brand-new pediatric emergency department.

continued on page 24

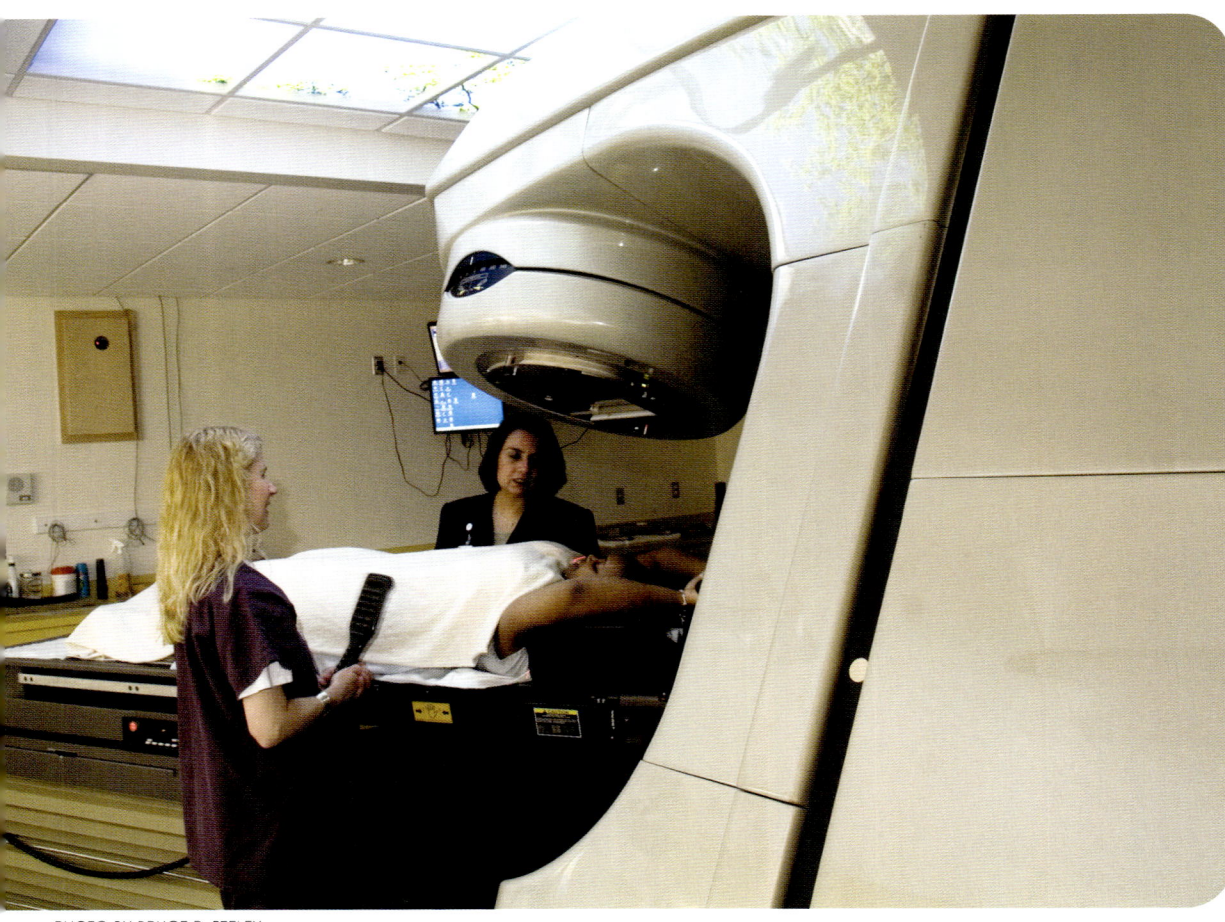

The Mary Elizabeth Miller Radiation Oncology Center at Inova Loudoun Hospital uses equipment that enables physicians to localize treatment areas accurately. In addition to treatment, the hospital also provides education and support for patients and families in a warm environment.

PHOTO BY BRUCE R. FEELEY

continued from page 23

emergency medicine. From a child-friendly waiting room with toys and games, to the special touch of a hand to hold, every consideration is given to the needs of children.

The Surgery Center is served by experienced doctors, dedicated nurses, and anesthesia professionals who realize that quality patient care is about more than a proper diagnosis and medication. It is also about strict protocols that ensure patients' comfort, safety, and above all confidence.

As a patient is having a renal arteriogram, the technologist can document the progress from the control room. Inova Loudoun Hospital uses the latest in state-of-the-art equipment, such as this Philips FD20 with GE Centricity monitoring system.

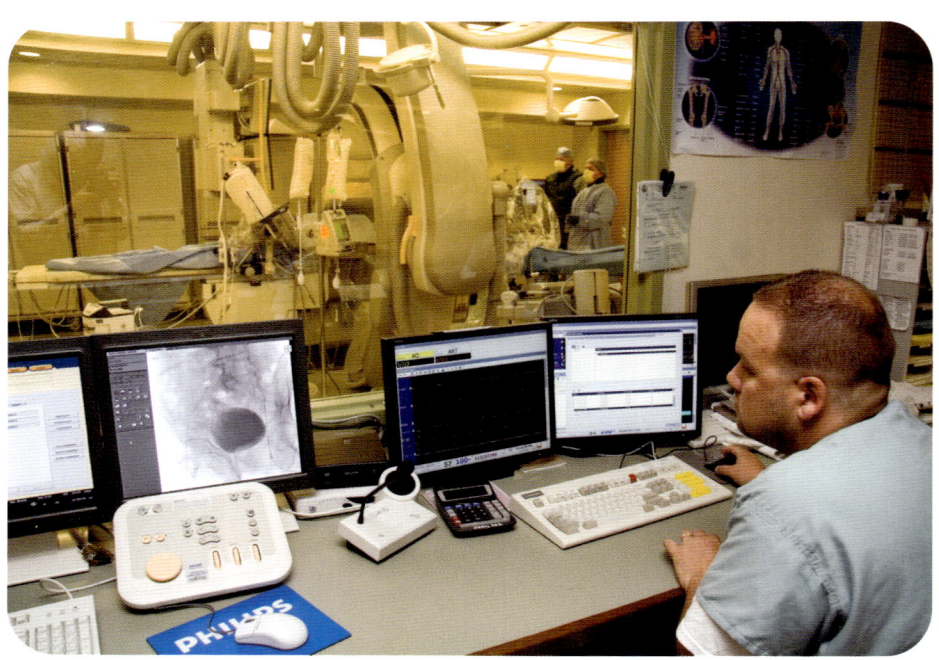

PHOTO BY BRUCE R. FEELEY

Patients in the cardiac rehab program at Inova Loudoun Hospital enjoy themselves while they exercise and improve their heart health.

PHOTO BY BRUCE R. FEELEY

The Physical Medicine and Rehabilitation Department covers physical and occupational therapy, speech pathology (including swallowing evaluation and treatment), pediatric rehab services, massage therapy, lymphedema/edema management, and wound care treatment.

Loudoun's Mobile Health Services bring health care to communities throughout the county and surrounding areas. The forty-foot van offers flu shots, as well as screenings for blood pressure, hearing, vision, glucose, bone density, and cholesterol. The van is also available for health fairs for local businesses.

Many of the doctors, nurses, and staff are local residents, making Inova Loudoun Hospital truly a community hospital. Their spirit goes beyond medicine. ✦

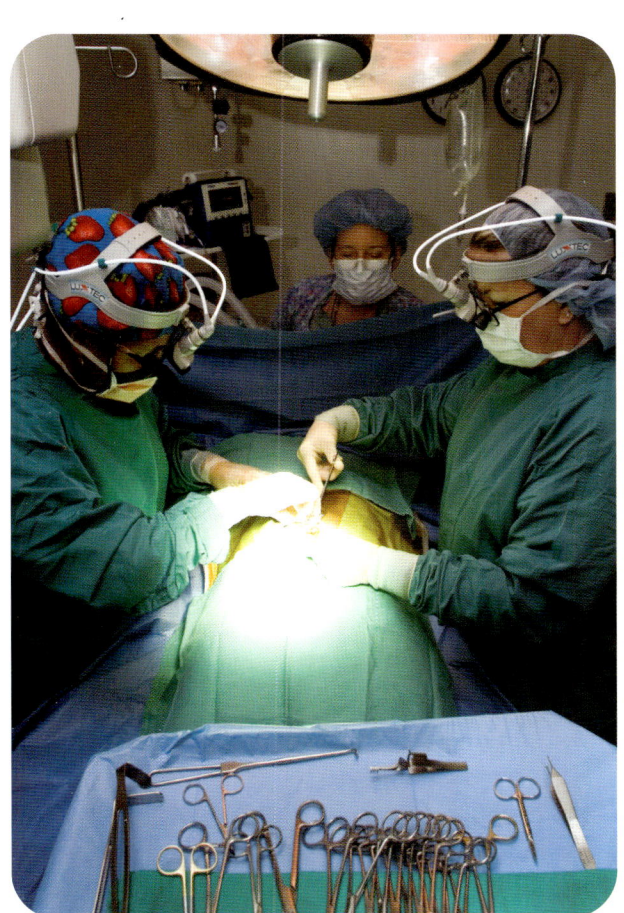

PHOTO BY BRUCE R. FEELEY

Inova Loudoun Hospital offers a wide variety of surgical services provided by highly skilled surgical specialists, ranging from general and laparoscopic techniques to more advanced procedures. Claudine Humphrey, Terry Trail, and Jan Pumphrey, all RN first assistants, use their skills and training to prepare a patient for surgery.

It has been said that horses are the unsung heroes in our history. When the first colonists arrived in Jamestown, Virginia, they brought horses with them. Horses helped early colonists farm the land, carried the pioneers as they explored the frontier, and pulled barges along rivers, wagons along dirt roads, and cannons into battle. During the Civil War, more horses than soldiers lost their lives. Horses such as Seabiscuit became famous sports figures, and mounted police still patrol our city streets. Today Loudoun County has the largest horse population in the state and the third-largest in the nation. Foxhunting, steeplechase races, Thoroughbred breeding, horse farms, and horseback riding contribute significantly to Virginia's wealth. Loudoun County has been described by travel writer Sharon Cavileer as "the Old Dominion in riding breeches." The Upperville Colt and Horse Show held each June near Middleburg is the oldest horse show in the country. Wherever they may be found, horses are linked to Virginia's heritage and to its future.

PHOTO BY JEANETTE BURKLE

Keeping Pace with Change

A bright future planted in rich soil

In the late 1800s, the rich soil in Loudoun County made it the fourth-largest wheat provider in the United States. Agriculture was still the dominant way of life in the 1920s when the Leesburg Chamber of Commerce was formed. But in the early '60s, the new Dulles International Airport signaled the beginning of a profound change in the way of life of the county.

In the last three decades, the population of Loudoun County has nearly quadrupled, and global corporations have now settled into Loudoun's bucolic landscape. Today, the county's still-vibrant agricultural economy operates in close proximity to glittering corporate campuses.

"Loudoun County has seen some remarkable growth over the last two generations, and the Loudoun County Chamber of Commerce has done an outstanding job in keeping pace with those changes to ensure this community maintains a competitive business climate and world-class quality of life," said Tony Howard, president of the chamber. "In order to keep pace with the changing business landscape, we've expanded the scope of our services to include programs of interest to the larger corporations and global companies that are located in our area." These include companies such as AOL, Verizon, and Orbital Sciences Corporation.

"It's a wonderful mixture," Howard said. "Members who do business out of their home offices serve on committees alongside business leaders from the major players."

The opening in 1995 of the Greenway—a thirteen-mile toll road connecting Dulles to Leesburg—also contributed to the county's residential growth.

Throughout the years, the Loudoun Chamber has maintained a strong voice in public policy at both the state and local levels. It also participates in the life of the community in a number of unique ways. "We're the last chamber in northern Virginia that hosts a consumer expo for our members," said Howard. The annual event, held at the Dulles Town Center, the county's most upscale retail destination, gives chamber members an opportunity to put their products and services in front of a highly desirable audience. "For anyone with a consumer focus, this is a chance to develop leads for the entire year," said Howard

Another unique project developed and promoted by the chamber was "Horsing Around Loudoun," a countywide public arts display that was recognized with a Signatures of Loudoun Award in 2006. Twenty-five life-sized sculptures of whimsically decorated horses were installed in public places around the county for just over six months. "It was the first event of its kind in Loudoun, and the public loved it," said Howard. The horses were created by local artists and auctioned at the end of the exhibit at a gala held at historic Oatlands Plantation.

The Loudoun Chamber will continue to change as this historic county grows and evolves. "That's what we're here for," said Howard. "I wouldn't have it any other way." ✦

Fanciful horses from the Chamber's Horsing Around Loudoun public arts program were auctioned at historic Oatlands Plantation in March 2006.

"The Loudoun County Chamber of Commerce has done an outstanding job to ensure this community maintains a competitive business climate and world-class quality of life."

Joseph Pozzo, chief, Loudoun County Department of Fire, Rescue & Emergency Management, awarded firefighter John Meyers the Meritorious Action Award during the Chamber's 2006 Valor Awards for helping save a resident and extinguish a rapidly spreading apartment fire.

PHOTO BY DAVE GALEN

From colorful macaws to pot-bellied pigs, an intriguing mix of animals awaits visitors to Leesburg Animal Park. The park invites children and adults to pet and feed many of the animals, such as rabbits and sheep, while others, like water buffalo and serval cats, are best observed from afar. Below: Lynette Olifer with son Charlie, age four, get a close encounter with the park's goats. The park can also make special arrangements to bring its domestic and exotic animals to area events and schools in order to provide hands-on learning experience.

Many Loudoun County residential developments, like this one in Leesburg, are governed by covenants that preserve both the historic character of the buildings and the area's small-town feel.

PHOTO BY THOMAS S. ENGLAND

Respect…Good Business Depends on It

Guidance and support in your professional development

Ask anyone involved in the real estate industry, and they'll tell you their job isn't about selling homes; it's about helping people achieve a part of the American Dream. For nearly half a century, the Dulles Area Association of REALTORS®, Inc. (DAAR) has facilitated that dream by providing education and support to real estate professionals throughout Loudoun County.

Established via charter in 1962, DAAR incorporated as the Loudoun County Board of REALTORS® in August 1969 with five firms and the area's first Multiple Listing Service. The association changed its name in 1994 to better reflect its market area, and today DAAR has grown to include 200 firms, 1,500 REALTOR® members, and 230 affiliate members.

While it has grown over the years, DAAR's mission has remained constant: to advance professional services to its members and the public they serve.

"We remember every day that we are in the people business," says CEO Jeanette Newton. "So we treat our members as individuals and give them individualized service. Providing these opportunities for our members allows them to become the most effective and knowledgeable REALTORS® possible for their clients."

REALTORS® Chip Dodson, Rick Cockrill, H. B. Kilgour, and R. W. Gibson show support for their community by raising money for Loudoun Habitat for Humanity at their Annual Golf Tournament. Over the last fifteen years DAAR has donated more than $150,000 to various community charities.

Services include everything from networking events to classes covering the latest technologies to two Real Estate Stores at which members can purchase items to enhance their business and effectively market their services. The association also helps its members stay up-to-date on all the latest technologies, including how to build eye-catching and effective Web sites to meet the demands of a whole new generation of buyers.

"Ten years ago, we didn't need to instruct our members on how often to check their e-mail," says Newton. "Today, we're providing a host of educational opportunities to bring our members in line with new technologies and the computer-literate generation's expectations of instant information and responses."

In fact, as Newton points out, continuing education is a part of every REALTOR®'s professional life. "We're an industry that constantly self-regulates, and many people don't realize the amount of continuing education required of us—especially when it comes to ethics." New members are given a two-day ethics and orientation class that covers the codes set forth by the National Association of REALTORS®, and all members are kept up-to-date on changes to that code.

Promoting a positive industry image is of vital importance to DAAR. "We work very hard to raise the level of that image, and we're doing it by focusing on professionalism over production," says Newton.

Members are encouraged to join DAAR's Professional Honor Society, where they earn points toward membership based not only on production numbers, but also on professional development and community service.

continued on page 34

"We remember every day that we are in the people business."

The association endeavors to provide a wide range of educational opportunities for its members and the public. Its new, modern, sixty-two-student classroom at the Dulles Airport Office offers courses from safety training to ongoing, required ethics training, and certifications.

PHOTO BY JEANETTE BURKLE

REALTORS® gather with community-related industries at their Annual Expo and Conference at Lansdowne Resort. The conference includes seminars, the trade show, and a variety of networking events.

PHOTO BY JEANETTE BURKLE

continued from page 33

Regular participation in real estate–related organizations and activities is also encouraged. A founding shareholder of the Metropolitan Regional Information System, established in 1995, DAAR is also affiliated with both the National Association of REALTORS® and the Virginia Association of REALTORS®, with three of its members since 1975 serving as that organization's president.

To help benefit the community at large, DAAR and its members lend a helping hand to dozens of local and regional endeavors, including Christmas in April, the Good Shepherd Alliance, Loudoun Habitat for Humanity, and the Loudoun Abused Women's Shelter. In fact, the charitable auction it started in 1992 to benefit the shelter has grown to include six different regional charities, including the Loudoun Therapeutic Riding Foundation. In 2006, DAAR's work for the foundation was recognized with a prestigious Mellon-Corning Award.

Whether helping a real estate professional provide the best possible service or lending a hand to a worthy cause, each and every day the Dulles Area Association of REALTORS® has a positive impact on the people of Loudoun County. ✦

Association political advocacy at work: Tom Jewell (left), 2005 Virginia Association of REALTORS® president and 1998 president of the Dulles Area Association of REALTORS®, welcomes State Senator Mark Herring to DAAR's annual Legislative Meet and Greet as Sean Dunn looks on.

PHOTO BY ALAN S. WEINER

Oh, to be little again and dance to the rhythm of your heart. Ballet. Jazz. Tap. It's all about being able to don the leotard, tights, and shoes; pin the hair back; and twirl, bend, or shuffle to the music. And at the Encore Dance Studio, where these young dancers encounter the joy of physical expression, it's all about fun first, then exercise, education, performance, and finally, competition. Mix all those steps together, and you have a well-choreographed experience that teaches far more than dance.

Founded about 1733 by Amos Janney, a Quaker from Bucks County, Pennsylvania, the Town of Waterford eventually grew into the second-largest town in Loudoun County. But unlike many villages in the area, Waterford did not experience an economic boom after the Civil War. Nonetheless, that turned out to be a good thing, since few of the old buildings and homes were demolished to make way for new development. By 1937, a Historic American Buildings Survey was completed in Waterford, prompting many residents to purchase and restore the town's old homes and other buildings. In 1943, these residents established the Waterford Foundation with the mission to "revive and stimulate a community interest in re-creating the town of Waterford as it existed in previous times with its varying crafts and activities." In 1970, the town and 1,420 surrounding acres were designated a National Historic Landmark.

PHOTO BY THOMAS S. ENGLAND

PHOTO BY BRUCE R. FEELEY

History … An Amazing Storyteller

Reveal the mystery at Thomas Balch Library

If libraries are repositories of all things literary, then Thomas Balch Library is the custodian of community memories. As a history and genealogy library, it plays a unique and vital role in the life of Leesburg.

"I think it's the jewel in the crown of Leesburg, actually," says Deborah Lee, Ph.D., an independent scholar and historian who is also a consultant for the Black History Committee of the Friends of the Thomas Balch Library. The history of the Leesburg/Loudoun County area is particularly rich, and in each room of the library researchers will discover resources to facilitate their undertakings in this region of Virginia. Personal papers of families of the area, town and business records, and church documents are all available. Collections are in many formats: books, periodicals, newspapers, manuscripts, maps, photographs, and microfilm.

"People tend to think of archives as dry, and librarians as the guardians," says Lee. "But on the contrary, the [Thomas] Balch [Library] is like a treasure house, and the librarians and staff are there to help find the treasure you're looking for

in your research." Such treasures focus on Loudoun County, regional and Virginia history, genealogy, and military history — with special emphasis on the American Civil War — and ethnic history.

The library was dedicated in 1922 by Edwin Swift Balch and Thomas Willing Balch to honor their father's memory in the town of his birth. Thomas Balch (1821–1877), a noted attorney of his day, was also a keen student of history throughout his life, and involved with a number of historical societies. He is known as the "Father of International Arbitration" for his efforts at the close of the Civil War, in proposing a plan to resolve the "Alabama Claims," which resulted in a $15.5 million settlement for the United States against Great Britain. Averaging between fifteen thousand and seventeen thousand visitors a year, Thomas Balch Library is a popular destination for visitors in an area where myriad places await discovery for newcomers or simply rediscovery for those who have visited previously.

The library is owned and operated by the Town of Leesburg and receives support from the nonprofit Friends of the Thomas Balch Library, Inc., as well as the community at large. "The community fought to preserve the library," explains Alexandra Gressitt, director. "With so much history, it is central to the community." Not only is the library unusual in its category as a specialized library owned by a municipality, Gressitt also notes that it is unusual because it is so dear to the hearts of many. "Because this town has taken such care to maintain the library and to move it forward, it reflects the quality of life that we enjoy here in Leesburg." ✦

"The [Thomas] Balch [Library] is like a treasure house, and the librarians and staff are there to help find the treasure you're looking for in your research."

The stately columns fronting the now-ceremonial entrance of Thomas Balch Library are original to the building, designed by noted Washington, D.C., architect Waddy B. Wood. In 2000 a new two-floor addition doubled the library's size, allowing for expansion of its collections and creating meeting space for community groups.

From "Beginning Genealogy" to "Notable Women in Northern Virginia's Past," Thomas Balch Library offers classes, lectures, and exhibits. Under the watchful gaze of Thomas Balch, staff members provide assistance to genealogists, historians, students, and members of the community conducting research using the library's collection of books, manuscripts, and other materials.

PHOTO BY BRUCE R. FEELEY

PHOTO BY ALAN S. WEINER

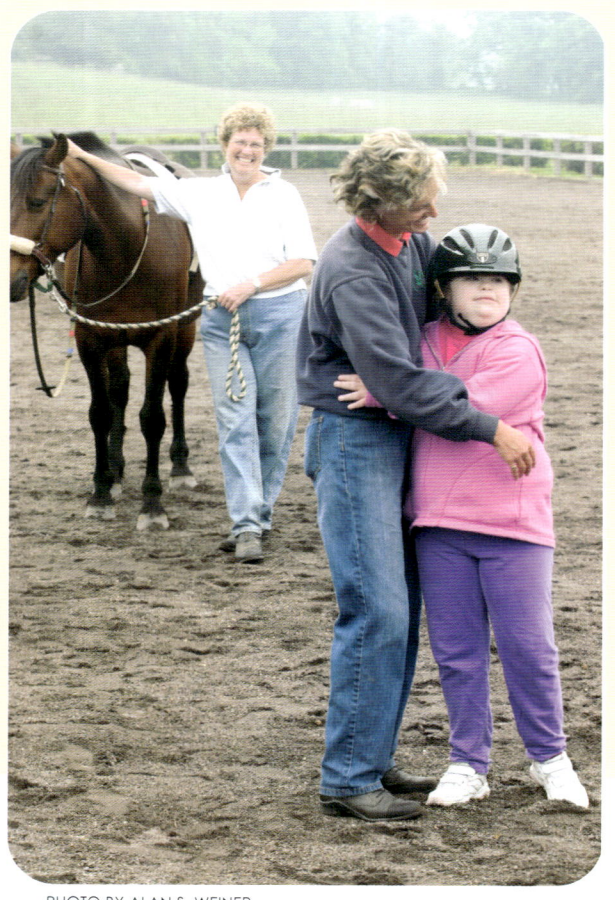

For over three decades, the Loudoun Therapeutic Riding Foundation has provided horseback riding opportunities to children and adults with disabilities. Through the foundation's programs, people with a range of disabilities can gain a heightened level of functionality that helps with their daily living activities. From building confidence to improving muscle strength and flexibility, therapeutic riding and tending to horses have proven to be highly beneficial forms of recreational therapy. Conducted under the guidelines of the North American Riding for the Handicapped Association, the foundation's programs employ certified instructors, volunteers, and special equipment to assist clients with a variety of physical and cognitive impairments. The foundation is located at Morven Park, the historic twelve-hundred-acre estate of Virginia Governor Westmoreland Davis. Located just west of Leesburg, the estate features beautifully manicured grounds and a magnificent turn-of-the-century mansion.

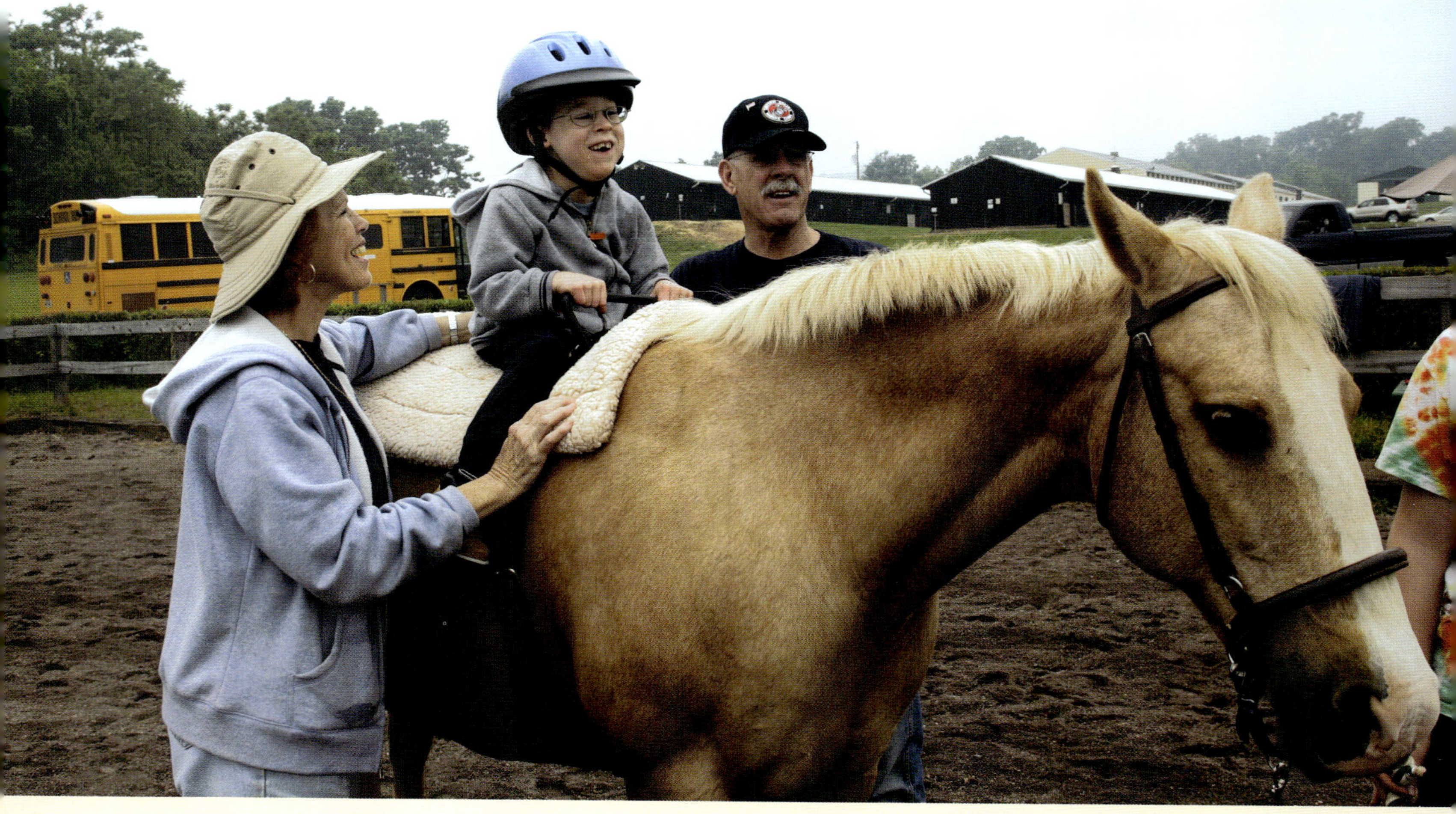

PHOTO BY ALAN S. WEINER

When Grace Keenan and the Nova Medical Group staff heard about Walking for Water, a nonprofit that helps the African village of Dagara build wells for fresh drinking water by using a combination of Western technology and village wisdom, they felt a kinship with the organization and a desire to help. So, Nova gladly sponsored a Walking for Water fund-raiser in May 2006.

PHOTO BY JEANETTE BURKLE

Loudoun Cares is an organization that strives to "create and sustain an innovative nonprofit human service center that includes comprehensive information and referral services benefiting Loudoun residents." In a special effort to help families with rising heating fuel costs, NEW Customer Service Companies, Inc. presented Loudoun Cares with a five-thousand-dollar donation at its corporate headquarters in Dulles. The need for assistance was well publicized, stating that households heating primarily with natural gas could expect to spend 48 percent more during the winter season. Andy Johnston, executive director of Loudoun Cares, made an appeal to businesses and religious organizations. NEW led the way in helping to raise awareness, and many corporations and congregations pitched in to help out.

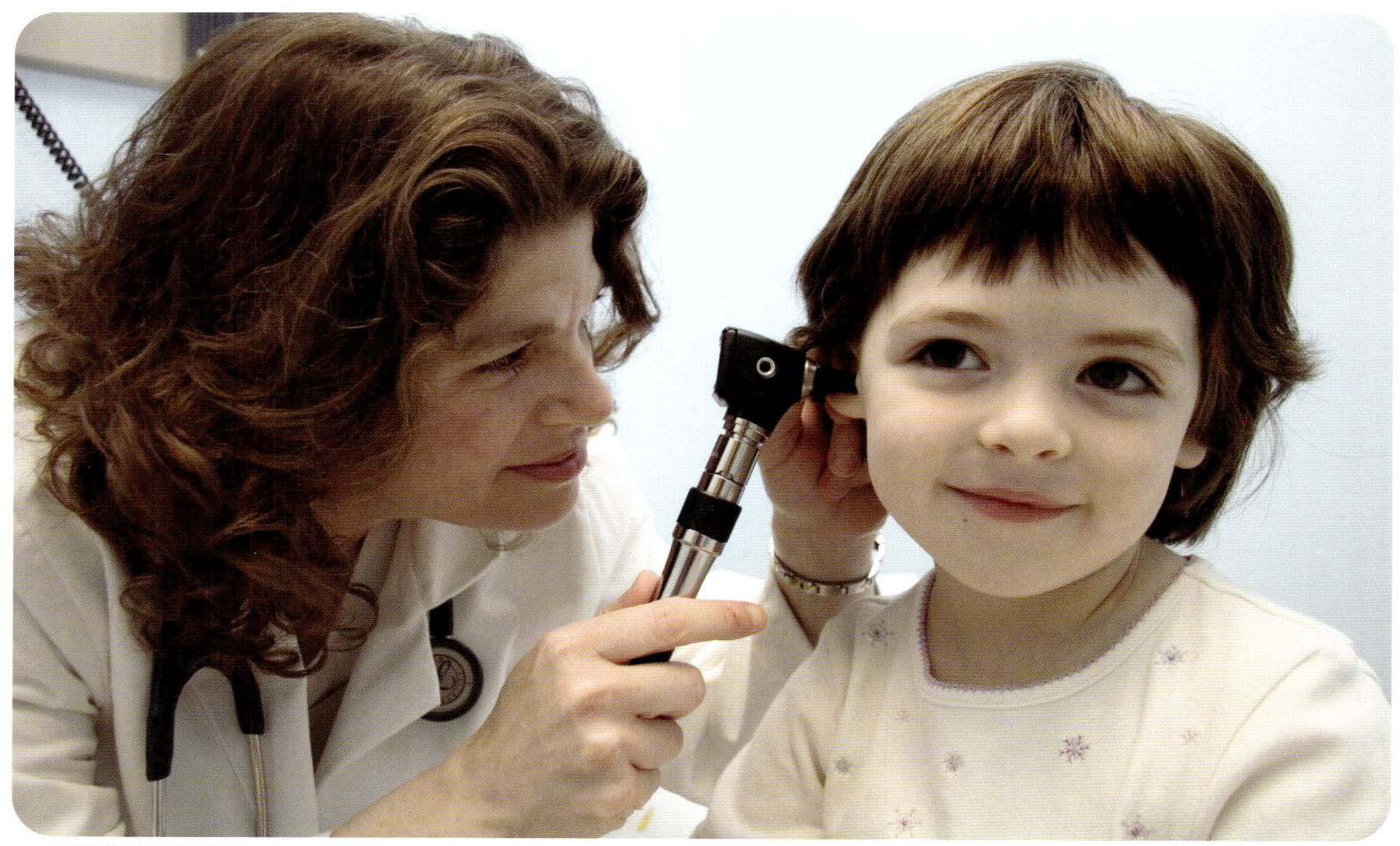

PHOTO BY BRUCE R. FEELEY

Beyond the Basics

Ensuring genuine wellness with comprehensive care

NOVA MEDICAL GROUP & URGENT CARE CENTER, INC.

Founded in 1988 by Grace L. Keenan, M.D., in Sterling, Virginia, Nova Medical Group has expanded to four locations including Leesburg, Warrenton, and Ashburn. Nova blends traditional Western medicine focusing on procedural, laboratory, and prescription medication interventions with complementary medicine, including naturopathic and Oriental medicine, acupuncture, biofeedback, mind-body medicine, hypnosis, hydrotherapy, massage, nutritional counseling, and personal training. This unique approach places self-care central to health care, allowing patients more involvement in their medical management and choice in their path to wellness. At Nova, patients have access to management options targeting the causes of illness, minimizing their impact on the individual, and maximizing wellness. "We have increased the tools in the toolbox and given more control to patients," explains medical director Keenan. "A traditional approach is taken in diagnosing and evaluating patients. In addition to customary approaches including procedures and prescription medications, we offer other alternatives."

A patient with high cholesterol may elect an herbal therapy before moving directly to a prescription drug. That individual would then work with his or her doctor to create a personalized program facilitating lifestyle changes, including nutritional counseling and weight loss, stress management techniques, and exercise. Lifestyle management modifications impact the entire body and improve most medical conditions, empowering patients with a new approach, and limiting the unnecessary costs and side effects of expensive drugs and procedures that would be used otherwise.

Patients young and old can find everything they need at Nova Medical Group. For little ones, Susanna Goheen, MD, FAAP, offers exceptional pediatric care in a way that makes young patients comfortable with the entire medical experience.

Each Nova location not only offers routine primary care, but also treatment for acute medical illnesses on a walk-in basis through its Urgent Care Centers, providing patients with more convenient, cost-effective care than found in a typical emergency room. According to Keenan, 80 percent of all patients who go to the emergency room could be handled in an urgent-care setting. In addition, the Urgent Care Centers offer ancillary services such as school and sports physicals, drug screenings, worker's compensation evaluations, immunizations, and more.

In January 2005, the Ashburn office became home to the Medical Spa at Nova, enhancing its services with new medically based spa offerings, such as massage therapy, hydrotherapy, detoxification protocols, laser hair removal, IPL, advanced signature cellulite treatments, Botox™, Restylane™, and customized fitness programs. Nova provides Loudoun County patients with truly comprehensive care supported by highly trained internal medicine, family practice, pediatric, and dermatology specialists, as well as nurse practitioners, naturopathic doctors, and multiple ancillary medical professionals.

The popularity of Nova's distinctive concept and superior customer service has led it to become the largest primary-care practice in the county. Keenan notes, "We want patients to feel they are listened to and receive individualized treatment, optimizing wellness."

continued on page 44

"We want patients to feel they are listened to and receive individualized treatment, optimizing wellness."

The waiting room of the medical group and urgent care center at Nova's main office in Ashburn provides and a warm and inviting environment for patients, complete with the friendly face and welcoming presence of concierge Donald Osborn.

PHOTO BY BRUCE R. FEELEY

Comfort and peacefulness are paramount at the Medical Spa at Nova. For that reason, the tranquility room—the homey, intimate "waiting room" where patients relax before or in between services—is designed to provide a sense of coziness and a genuine feeling of serenity.

PHOTO BY BRUCE R. FEELEY

continued from page 43

THE MEDICAL SPA AT NOVA

The Medical Spa at Nova, located in Ashburn, is a full-service medical spa. Unlike a traditional spa, the Medical Spa at Nova emphasizes preventative and restorative therapies, minimizing the need for more invasive and expensive approaches to wellness and anti-aging. Under the direction of medical doctors, a group of highly trained estheticians, massage therapists, fitness instructors, biofeedback specialists, acupuncturists, and naturopathic physicians individualize care for residents of Loudoun County. Medical-grade skin-care and bath products not found in typical day spas are available. Advanced skin-care technology, including VISIA™, provides an objective measurement of skin damage, wrinkles, and pore size for pre- and posttreatment analysis. Services include on-site dermatology, massage therapy, hydrotherapy, detoxification protocols, laser hair removal, IPL, advanced signature

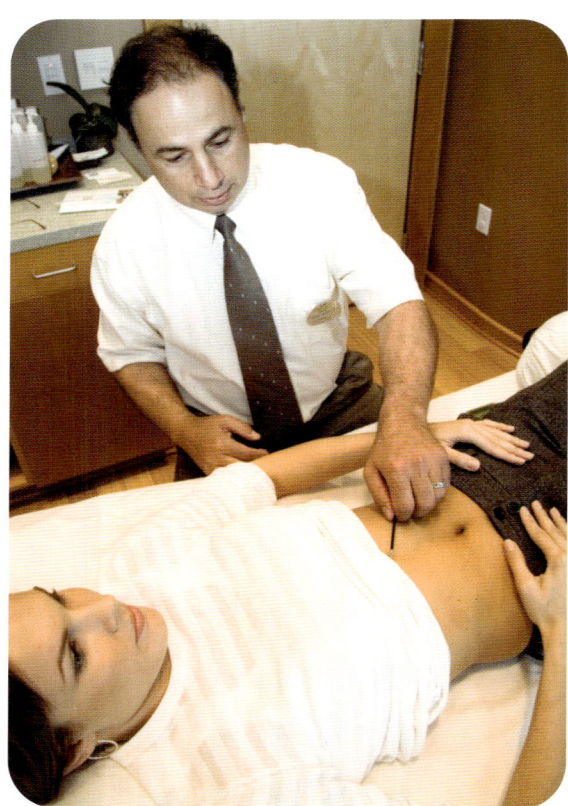

Offering a full range of complementary medicine is just one of the unique components that makes Nova Medical Group truly stand out in the local health-care community. Here, Michael Jabalee, LAc, works with incense as part of this patient's acupuncture treatment.

PHOTO BY BRUCE R. FEELEY

Working together to help patients find the treatments that are right for them is a key element for the entire staff at Nova. Pictured here (from left to right), Rhonda Mough, MD; medical director and founder Grace Keenan, MD; Holger Noelle, MD; and Darleen Mowry, MA, meet at the center's nursing station to consult for a few moments about the day's cases.

PHOTO BY BRUCE R. FEELEY

cellulite treatments, Botox™, Restylane™, a nonsurgical facelift, facial acupuncture, sclerotherapy, and customized fitness programs. Nova's services are intended to provide more benefit than typical aesthetic treatments. Nova's goal is to assist people in making healthy life choices, rejuvenating the body, reinforcing an individual's overall wellness, and enhancing appearance.

"Adding the spa gave Nova a healing environment to perform and integrate naturopathic and traditional medicine. Hydrotherapy tubs promoting lymphatic drainage and infrared sauna are necessary for detoxification protocols," Dr. Keenan explains.

Services offered at the Medical Spa at Nova frequently accompany the treatment regimens recommended by the medical providers who work within Nova Medical Group. All Loudoun County residents have access to the spa's numerous beneficial treatments. Nova features signature programs including Mind-Body Medicine, Smoking Cessation, Fibromyalgia Management, Bio Identical Hormone Therapy, and a Fitness and Nutrition Program. Nova's unique medical spa allows a well-deserved day of relaxation in a beautiful, healing environment. ✦

By providing preventative and restorative therapies, the Medical Spa at Nova promotes health and wellness in addition to relaxation and repose. For instance, the hydrotherapy tub shown here can be used medically or as a rejuvenating escape. In either case, this client will not only walk away feeling better, but also very calm and rested.

PHOTO BY BRUCE R. FEELEY

Lunch or Anytime

* Entree Croissants
* Country Sandwiches
* Home Baked Bread / Rolls
* Barbque w/ Home Baked Roll
* Pasta Club Salad
* Soups
* Country Cookies & Bars

Smoothies 3.25

* Strawberry
* Peach * Banana
* Wildberry
* Cafe mocha
* Pina Colada * orange creme
* Raspberry * Mango

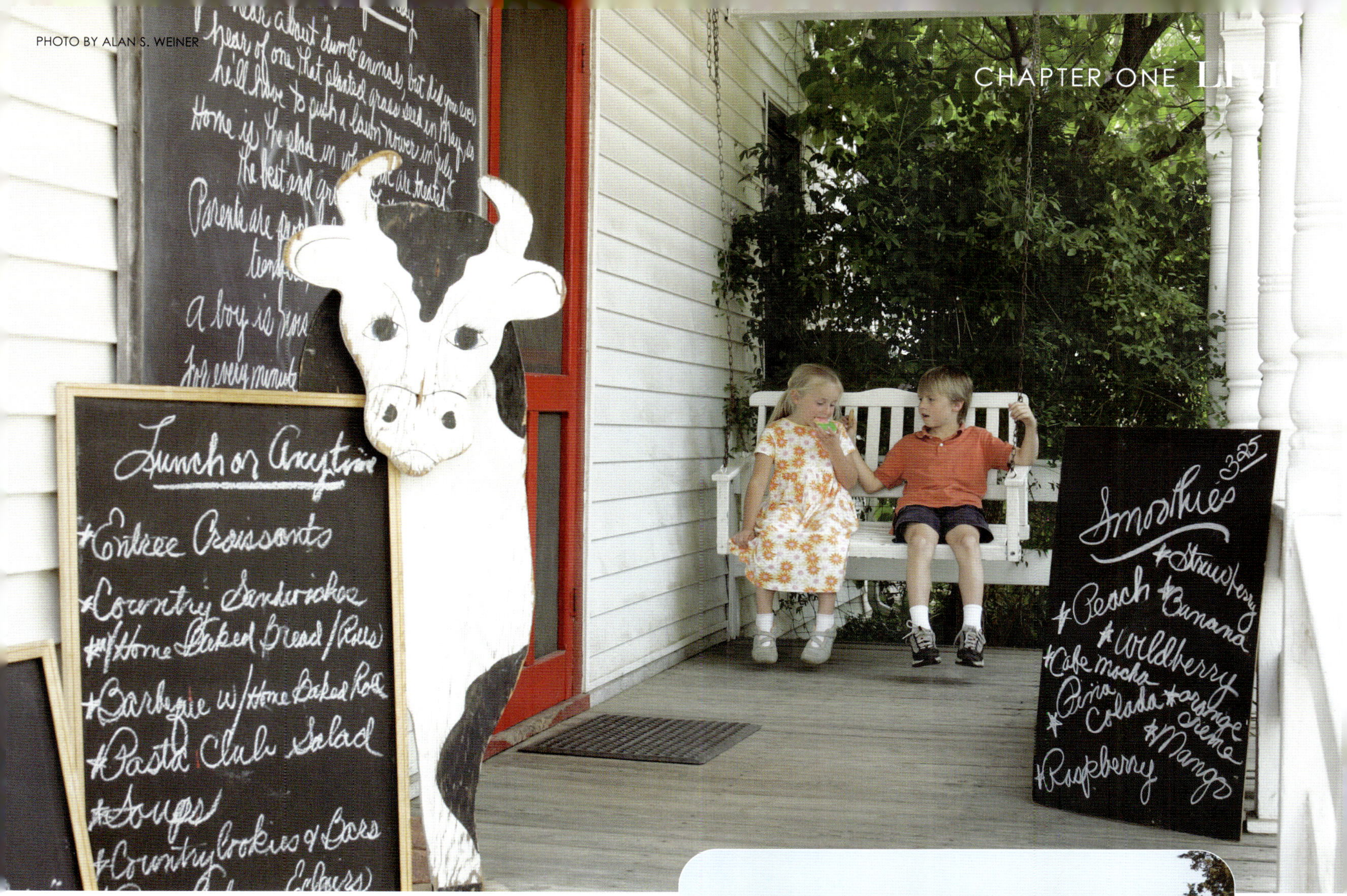

M iddleburg, on the southern edge of Loudoun County,
is a charming, centuries-old community place that a
few hundred Virginians now call home. Long a stopover along
the Ashby Gap Road, Middleburg is still home to a distinctive
collection of historic inns, including one of the nation's original
lodging establishments, the Red Fox Inn. The town itself has
retained much of its Colonial-era ambience, with elegant
galleries and shops now lining Washington Street, the town's
central avenue. Around the turn of the twentieth century,
Middleburg began to draw horse enthusiasts for foxhunting and
steeplechase events, earning the town its title as the capital of
horse country. Above: Sophie and Sam Coolidge know that one
of the best places to enjoy an afternoon on the porch swing is
at Scruffy's Ice Cream Parlor.

PHOTO BY DAVID GALEN

Progress . . . It's More Than You Imagine

Discover opportunities as diverse as the landscape

Located twenty-five miles from the nation's capital and bordered by the Blue Ridge Mountains and Potomac River, Loudoun County is known for its beautiful scenery, rich history, and strong sense of community. For over two centuries, it remained a predominantly agricultural community, but in recent decades has emerged as an international center for technology, communications, and transportation businesses, and has become one of the fastest-growing counties in the nation. Along the way, the Loudoun County government has played a key role in the region's progress and prosperity, working with innovative community partners and remaining committed to delivering top-notch services that ensure fiscal strength and an unparalleled quality of life.

With seven incorporated towns, eleven villages, and dozens of master-planned communities, Loudoun County offers more than 250,000 residents some of the best residential and employment opportunities in the region. As a result, Loudoun has consistently ranked near the top on national measures of economic stability and quality of life. Yearly analyses consistently show the county to have one of the highest median household incomes, while also achieving some of the lowest rates of unemployment and poverty nationwide. Appearing on numerous "Best Of" lists, Loudoun was also recently ranked fifth nationwide in overall "Best Quality of Life" by the *American City Business Journals*.

Jim Desy and his children, Matthew and Lydia, enjoy a taste of summer at the Tarara Winery Blackberry Days Wine Festival. The event includes wine tastings, u-pick blackberries, music, and crafts and food vendors, and is just one of many special events held annually at Loudoun's thirteen wineries. County winegrape production has increased 200 percent in the last five years, as soil and climate conditions, access to technical experts, and skilled winemakers have contributed to Loudoun's growing reputation as "wine country."

Loudoun is also one of the select counties in the nation to be awarded AAA bond ratings by the nation's three leading bond-rating agencies: Standard and Poor's, Moody's, and Fitch. When issuing its rating, Standard and Poor's cited Loudoun's "rapidly growing economic and employment base, continued strong tax base and employment growth . . . , one of the highest wealth and income levels of all U.S. counties, [and] strong financial performance and good reserves."

To remain fully attentive to the real-life demands of such a dynamic community, the Loudoun County government, under the direction of the nine-member Board of Supervisors and the county administrator, works to provide superior-level services and innovative programs. Recent initiatives include a significant expansion of commuter services to Washington, D.C.; ambitious youth initiative partnerships with public, private, and faith-based organizations; transportation improvements utilizing a $200 million design-build contract under Virginia's Public-Private Transportation Act; and a study of the potential for broadband service expansion throughout the county.

Hard work and innovation have been recognized, as county programs and departments are the frequent recipients of statewide and national awards. The Loudoun Management and Financial Services Department has received numerous national awards for excellence in

continued on page 50

The county government has been named as one of the ten most technologically advanced in the United States.

Young fans enjoy a warm afternoon watching their football heroes on the field. One of the many special entertainment options in Loudoun is free public access to Redskins training camps, held each summer at Redskins Park in Ashburn. Many of the professional players and their families also call Loudoun home, living in a number of the county's upscale residential neighborhoods.

PHOTO BY DAVID GALEN

Loudoun's distinctive towns and villages are known for historic homes, fine dining, and thriving entrepreneurial businesses. Each is also host to a variety of cultural activities, which span the range from bluegrass concerts, Civil War reenactments, and county fairs to point-to-point horse racing, hunt rides, juried arts and crafts competitions, and annual German Oktoberfest events. Here, visitors and residents flock to the annual Leesburg Flower & Garden Festival.

PHOTO BY ANN HIGGINS

continued from page 49

financial reporting. The county's Public Information Office has been selected as one of a handful nationwide to earn "Superior-level" awards for the county's annual report. The county government as a whole has been named three years in a row as one of the ten most technologically advanced in the United States by the Center for Digital Government. The county has also received several accolades from the Virginia Association of Counties, most recently recognizing the Department of Animal Care and Control's Companion Animal Resource Effort, and the Department of Parks, Recreation and Community Services' Athletic Space Allocation program.

The award-winning Atlantic Boulevard building at Dulles Town Center is one of Loudoun's most visible examples of Class A commercial space. Loudoun developers also offer businesses customized build-to-suit opportunities and a variety of existing industrial, flex, and office locations, all along well-planned commercial corridors.

PHOTO BY JIM KIRBY

Loudoun County also helps ensure the region's economic and cultural vitality by creating and nurturing public-private partnerships. Key among these are partnerships grown from the county's Department of Economic Development (DED), such as the Economic Development Commission and Rural Economic Development Council, working to promote both traditional business and agricultural niche industries while addressing specific goals laid forth in the community's strategic plan. One recently created partnership is the CEO Cabinet, a select group of executives from Loudoun's corporate and entrepreneurial firms, and nonprofit and government institutions, who address business, community, and quality-of-life topics. Another is the all-volunteer Design Cabinet, in which experts advise and reward communities for quality architectural and design development. The Main Street Loudoun Partnership, coordinated through DED, works to enhance commercial districts through its focus on business development, organization, design, and promotion, while DED's innovative Science and Technology Cabinet encourages development of the region as a global center for science- and technology-based businesses.

In addition to the high-quality services and careful guidance provided by the Loudoun County government and its partners, other assets contribute to the county's enviable quality of life. Dulles International Airport supplies ready access to the world, while the county's proximity to Washington, D.C., provides access to some of the nation's finest cultural and leisure attractions and the business-enhancing power of federal government spending. Closer to home, residents enjoy access to Loudoun's three diverse environments: rural landscapes; distinctive towns; and contemporary, thriving suburban developments. Of course, Loudoun's greatest asset will always be its people, whose dedication to the community help make it what it is today. ✦

Shire draft horses pull visitors at Ayrshire Farm, a premier Loudoun County working farm specializing in rare and endangered breeds of livestock as well as heirloom fruits and vegetables. The county's $295 million equine industry is the most valuable in the state, with the average per-head value of horses exceeding that of all other Virginia counties. The county's twenty-thousand-plus horses are used for trail riding, foxhunting, broodmare operations, equestrian show competitions, and racing.

PHOTO BY ANN HIGGINS

PHOTO BY DAVID GALEN

Really Great Finds
~ ANTIQUES & DECOR ~
540-338-7799
www.reallygreatfinds.com

Coffee
Now Open

When Suzanne Kidney opens her two-story home to antique lovers, a wealth of discovery awaits. Bottom right: Known as Really Great Finds, the Purcellville home and shop is a favorite browsing spot for friends Jennifer Jenkins, Julie Simpson, and Kim Kendall. Below: Catherine Abramson of Round Hill, Virginia, knows that from hats and bags to sofas and swags, there are thousands of items to peruse among the shop's consignors. Far left: For Caroline Abramson, a bit of old-fashioned bling is the perfect find. When the shop is closed, outdoor items can be purchased at the store's Blackberry Gourmet Coffee Kiosk. A second Really Great Finds shop is just up the road in Lucketts.

PHOTO BY DAVID GALEN

PHOTO BY DAVID GALEN

PHOTO BY NICHOLAS TAN

Inquiry ... The Lifelong Habit of the Mind

Extending academic excellence outward into the world

Rooted in Virginia's strong tradition of educational excellence and dedicated to meeting the present and future needs of a growing and diverse student body, George Mason University shines as the region's foremost institution of higher learning.

George Mason University traces its roots back to 1957 when a resolution passed by the Commonwealth of Virginia established a branch college of the University of Virginia in the city of Fairfax. That college, George Mason College of the University of Virginia, was established as a four-year, degree-granting institution with the mandate to eventually expand into a major university. On April 7, 1972, the Virginia General Assembly enacted legislation that allowed George Mason to separate from its parent institution and operate as an independent member of Virginia's system of colleges and universities.

Since that time, George Mason has grown to serve the entire northern Virginia region, currently operating campuses in Arlington, Fairfax, and Prince William County, with a temporary site in Loudoun County that will expand into a full campus by 2009.

What draws students to George Mason is its emphasis on diversity and innovation, which allows for a broad range of intellectual exploration and growth within some of the finest academic programs in the country. Ranked among the

When it was dedicated in 1996, the Johnson Center was the first building of its kind on an American campus to feature, all in one building, academic and research facilities, student services, and a food court.

most diverse universities in the nation by the *Princeton Review*, George Mason boasts a student body from all fifty states and 168 countries. Out of a total of nearly 31,000 students, approximately 1,740 are registered as international students.

The university also draws prominent scholars from throughout the nation and the world, including economic science Nobel laureates James Buchanan and Vernon Smith, and the Robinson Professors, a group of outstanding scholars committed to undergraduate teaching and interdisciplinary scholarship. Faculty also includes Pulitzer Prize winners, several IEEE Centennial Medalists, and recipients of numerous grants and awards from Fulbright, the National Science Foundation, and the National Endowment for the Arts, among others.

Noted throughout the world for outstanding academic programs, George Mason boasts dozens of undergraduate degree options as well as several research centers, collaborative programs, and highly regarded postgraduate programs ranging from the liberal arts to technology and science.

Standouts include the George Mason University School of Law, ranked thirty-seventh in the United States; the industrial/ organizational psychology graduate program, which is consistently ranked in the top ten in the nation; and the School of Management, which, of over 2,500 business schools worldwide, is one of only

continued on page 56

George Mason University shines as the region's foremost institution of higher learning.

Patriot pride ran high in March 2006 as the men's basketball team set a number of records with its run to the NCAA Final Four. Although the Patriots eventually lost to the Florida Gators, they rank as the first Colonial Athletic Association (CAA) team—and the first true mid-major conference team since 1979—to crash the Final Four.

PHOTO BY EVAN CANTWELL

Located adjacent to Mason Pond, the university's Center for the Arts attracts more than one hundred thousand patrons each year to its world-class performances. As part of George Mason's College of Visual and Performing Arts, the center hosts performances by local artists, students, and faculty; the award-winning Theater of the First Amendment; and the Great Performances at Mason series.

PHOTO BY EVAN CANTWELL

continued from page 55

166 schools to be accredited in both business and accounting by the prestigious Association to Advance Collegiate Schools of Business International (AACSB). In 2005 *U.S. News & World Report* ranked the School of Management among the top 25 percent of all AACSB-accredited business schools.

Although not yet fully established at a permanent site, George Mason's Loudoun campus is following in those esteemed academic footsteps with five undergraduate programs in business and management, education and human development, health science, information technology, and social work. Graduate programs are offered in business administration, education and human development, nursing, and telecommunications.

By expanding its presence into Loudoun County, George Mason brings its rich history of academic excellence and diversity into one of the fastest-growing populations in the country. And in creating a vital educational, cultural, and economic resource for the region, this partnership adds yet another dimension to the high quality of life that defines Loudoun County. ✦

In May 2006 George Mason University celebrated the largest graduating class in the Commonwealth of Virginia and conferred nearly seven thousand undergraduate and graduate degrees.

PHOTO BY EVAN CANTWELL

Below, Loudoun schoolteacher Steve Martin observes his students as they investigate a series of specimens at the Smithsonian Naturalist Center in Leesburg. Loudoun County Public Schools (LCPS) is one of the fastest-growing school districts in the nation, serving over fifty thousand students, and the Smithsonian Naturalist Center, owner of the largest publicly accessible natural history reference collection in the country, is just one of its significant partners. Other unique programs include the School-Business Partnership, through which hundreds of Loudoun organizations such as Dulles Town Center, Virginia Concrete, and the Washington Redskins provide schools with direct financial support, mentoring, tutoring, supplies, exposure to career fields, and scholarships. Other LCPS partnerships include the Howard Hughes Medical Institute, which awards scholarships and runs the Academy of Science at Dominion High School, and AOL, which provides scholarships and annual grants through its Aspirations Fund program.

PHOTO BY ANN HIGGINS

Customers who seek freshly grown regional produce know to head to Heider's Country Store and Farm Market. Located on Route 15 five miles north of Leesburg and owned and operated by Albert Heider, the store features local produce and fresh flowers from growers throughout the county and the region, including the Pennsylvania Amish. Heider himself grows hard-to-find and heirloom fruits and vegetables, plus a variety of houseplants and cut flowers, which he also sells at his market. Open from April through the end of October, the market also features a variety of canned jams, jellies, and vegetables, plus crafts and other gifts.

Sweet Cherry
$ 4.29 box | Local
Sour Cherries | North Carolina
White Peaches

PHOTO BY THOMAS S. ENGLAND

MELONS

PHOTO BY ALAN S. WEINER

Home Ownership . . . The American Dream

Journey to your destination's end at Severn Mortgage

What's in a name? If you're Lawrie Vick and Cliff Warrington of Severn Mortgage, everything. For this husband-and-wife team, their company's name reflects those things they value most in life: family, lasting relationships, and commitment to excellence in serving their customers. The company name, "Severn," is the name of their son and of the longest river in England, where the family's ancestry lies, and their logo is a symbol for journey, movement, destination, and dreams—everything that defines the home-buying experience.

Privately owned and operated by Lawrie and Cliff since 1998, Severn Mortgage is in the business of turning the American Dream of home ownership into a reality. "Homes are real places, where families live and grow," says Cliff. "Where do we want to be at the end of the day? We want to be home. That's our goal, helping people arrive at that destination."

In an increasingly competitive market, where even homebuilders have their own mortgage arms, Severn stands out by combining the products of a national mortgage firm with the personalized service of a hometown business.

"We're competitive with all the national firms in that we offer the same rates, the same products," says Lawrie. "But there's a difference. We're local, and we're accessible. That means if you need something, you can walk right into our office and we'll take care of you immediately."

No matter the transaction—first home, refinance, or investment —Severn Mortgage expertly guides its clients through the entire loan process, from initial home loan application on through to closing.

"We're more than just a mortgage banker," Lawrie continues. "We like to think of ourselves as financial consultants. We have a tremendous sense of responsibility to our clients, and we really do go the extra mile."

With two locations and a team of twenty-five mortgage professionals, Severn offers the most up-to-date loan programs available — everything from conventional to jumbo, FHA to VA, Fannie Mae to Freddie Mac. "Staying current with what's going on in the market, knowing what the new product options are, that keeps us very connected," says Lawrie. "We specialize in alternative programs that serve those who don't necessarily fit into the typical mold."

To help extend that sense of family out into the community, the couple also donates their time and resources to dozens of local and regional charities and organizations. "If there's someone in the company who lives in a needy neighborhood or who has a child that goes to a school that needs help, we'll figure out a way to contribute," says Lawrie. "All people have to do is ask. If we can help out, we will."

That reciprocal relationship between business and community, says Cliff, is what makes Loudoun County such a special place. "Our goal is to continue to expand and provide opportunities for people while keeping the culture of a hometown business. I think that's why we've been so successful. This is a very tight-knit, supportive community. We really have to thank Loudoun County for helping us grow." ✦

The Severn Mortgage team of professional mortgage consultants is based in Leesburg, Virginia, and is proud to consistently be ranked as one of the best mortgage companies in Loudoun County. The team provides professional advice, client-centered service, a commitment to excellence, and a choice in home financing.

"We specialize in alternative programs that serve those who don't necessarily fit into the typical mold."

Cliff Warrington and Lawrie Vick, owners of Severn Mortgage, have built their company into a well-known and respected area business. They pride themselves on placing their clients at the center of their business and on giving back to the community through their charitable contributions, volunteer hours, and many sponsorships.

PHOTO BY ALAN S. WEINER

PHOTO BY SCOTT INDERMAUR

Stephen and Kelly Gaitten enjoy a glass of wine and the last rays of a summer sunset on the front porch of their Hamilton home. They bought the one-hundred-year-old Victorian and its three-acre lot in 2001 and immediately began renovations. "The porch was the first thing we worked on, because we knew we'd spend a lot of time out here," Kelly said. "We love renovating old houses because they just don't build houses like this anymore." In addition to the obvious charm of the house, the renovation turned up a secret room in the attic. Above: Not many people strolling along West Market Street would guess that the charming house with the inviting front porch was built in the 1800s. "This house and the one next door were both renovated in 2004," said Mervin Jackson, the present owner. "My wife, Jean, took one look at this house and insisted we buy it. The kitchen is brand-new, and she really likes the new screen porch and patio on the back." The house is made of an unusual mixture of pebbles mixed with mortar. The foundation and the wall out front are fieldstone.

PHOTO BY SCOTT INDERMAUR

Scientists Lead in New Directions

Our biomedical think tank turns "what if" into "what will be"

"What if?" It is a question mankind has asked since the beginning, and its implications for science, technology, and medicine are undeniable. If not for this simple question, there would be no laser, no transistor, no new microscopy methods, and no discovery of the structure of DNA. Unimaginable! These vital discoveries emerged from successful research organizations that encouraged blue-sky thinking in an environment that allowed scientists the freedom to follow new directions. Such is the mission of the Howard Hughes Medical Institute's Janelia Farm Research Campus in Loudoun County.

"One of the ways to describe Janelia Farm is as a start-up company whose product is new basic knowledge. Our mission is to do cutting-edge, long-range, adventuresome research," explains Gerald M. Rubin, an internationally recognized geneticist whose sole commitment now is to serve as mentor and leader to close to forty research groups who are equally as committed to the question of "what if?" In addition, Rubin adds, Janelia Farm's "investors" are very patient—a critical catalyst for optimal research outcomes.

Funded entirely by Howard Hughes Medical Institute (HHMI), scientists are free to concentrate on research without the constraints of grants, as often is the case in traditional academic research environments. "Howard Hughes Medical

Scientist Barret Pfeiffer prepares materials for testing in a newly opened laboratory at the Janelia Farm Research Campus.

Institute has always been guided by the principle of funding people, not projects," he says. In fact, in creating the Institute, Howard Hughes himself made certain that its aspirations were bold; its purpose, he said, was "to probe the genesis of life itself." Today, HHMI is a recognized leader in biomedical research, generating ideas that are improving the understanding of some of society's most vexing health problems, including AIDS, cardiovascular disease, and diabetes.

As HHMI's only freestanding campus, Janelia Farm will focus initially on the identification of general principles that govern how information is processed by neuronal circuits. According to Rubin, the long-term goal of understanding how the human brain works is, in his words, a hundred-year goal. "What we're doing at Janelia Farm is asking the question, 'If you wanted to achieve that goal in one hundred years, what would you do next Monday morning?' What we're doing is working on the very basic mechanism in much simpler systems than humans—worms, flies, and mice—to try and understand the basic rules," he explains. In addition, Janelia Farm will develop imaging technologies and computational analysis to enable precise examination of living cells. These two goals are naturally synergistic: to understand the functionality of the brain, it's essential to observe which neurons are active at which particular time, and that requires improving existing technologies for examining the activity of the nervous system.

continued on page 66

"Our mission is to do cutting-edge, long-range, adventuresome research."

Gerald M. Rubin, director of the Janelia Farm Research Campus, works closely with Cheryl Moore, the chief operating officer, to create a supportive and collaborative research environment.

PHOTO BY SCOTT INDERMAUR

The distinctive glass-enclosed auditorium is a focal point for many activities at the Janelia Farm Research Campus. HHMI president Thomas R. Cech, co-winner of the 1989 Nobel Prize for chemistry, is pictured here, at left, with Gerald M. Rubin, Janelia Farm's director.

PHOTO BY SCOTT INDERMAUR

continued from page 65

The genesis of the Janelia Farm Research Campus began with the observation that today's academic and industrial research models have become far too conservative and not collaborative enough. HHMI's planners carefully studied the structure and scientific culture of other important and highly successful research models, both at academic and for-profit biomedical laboratories, including the Medical Research Council Laboratory of Molecular Biology in England, and AT&T's Bell Laboratories in the United States. Though the two laboratories are different in many ways, they did have several things in common, which Janelia Farm is modeling: small research groups with principal scientists working at the bench, single-sponsor internal funding, and support services and infrastructure to support collaboration. As a result, everything about Janelia Farm is collaborative—from the architecture of the building that is shaped like an S and blends into the pastoral environs of Loudoun County, to the multidisciplinary teams of

Janelia Farm librarian Jeanne Fielding helps resident and visiting scientists in a technologically advanced setting that combines electronic and more traditional resources.

PHOTO BY SCOTT INDERMAUR

Left: The ground floor of the Janelia Farm Research Campus is paved with Italian balsatina stone, the same stone used in many parts of the Vatican in Rome. This view looking west reveals the glass and steel construction.

Below: The curving glass hallways in the Janelia Farm Research Campus blur the boundaries between the laboratories in the landscape building and the exterior landscape itself.

PHOTO BY SCOTT INDERMAUR

PHOTO BY SCOTT INDERMAUR

scientists who've earned their Ph.D. degrees in fields ranging from physics to chemistry, computer science to biophysics, molecular biology, and genetics.

The blue skies of Loudoun County seem to epitomize the blue-sky thinking of this extraordinary biomedical think tank. "Janelia Farm itself is an experiment in how to support the most creative scientists to get the largest output from them. Essentially, we're asking the scientists to bet their careers on their good ideas. In ten years, I see Janelia Farm as one of the most vibrant places to do basic biomedical research in the world," says Rubin. "We'll continue to attract the best people to come here, and we'll begin to see the fruit of this long-range work yielding tangible outcomes." In other words, Howard Hughes Medical Institute and Janelia Farm Research Campus are turning "what if?" into "what is possible." ✦

PHOTO BY ALAN S. WEINER

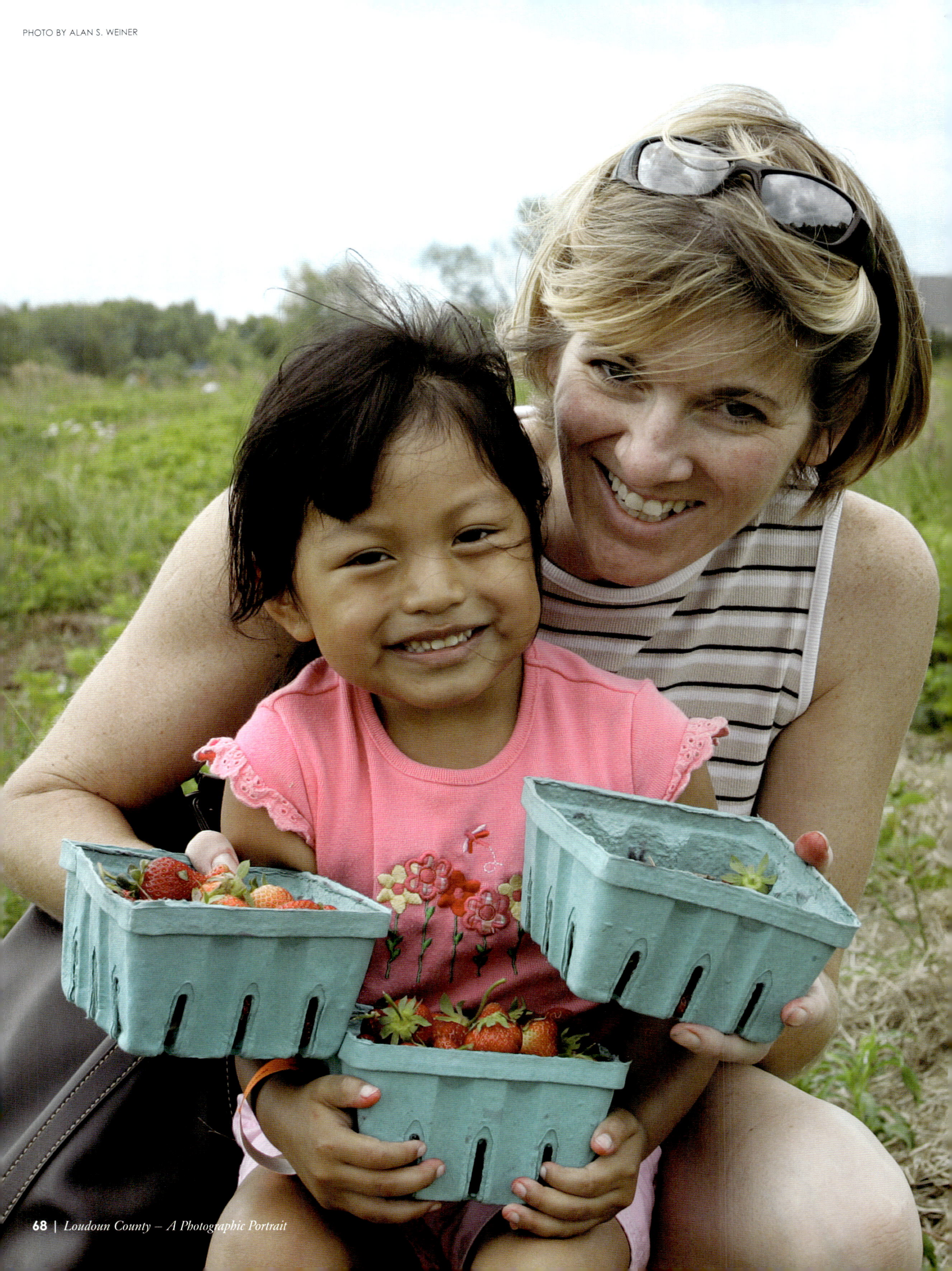

ooking for strawberries is a lot more fun than hunting Easter eggs, and they taste better. With big smiles and baskets overflowing, Colleen Dill and her daughter, Madison, agree. From strawberries and asparagus in the spring, to corn and tomatoes all summer, and then pumpkins and gourds in the fall, Great County Farms is a great way for families to enjoy farm life and go home with fresh fruits and vegetables. The farms cover two hundred acres at the base of the Blue Ridge Mountains outside the village of Bluemount, Virginia. Kids learn how food is grown and that fresh fruits and vegetables really taste good—no problem getting them to eat the produce they pick themselves. A trip to Great County Farms isn't all work, however. There is also time to feed the animals in the Farm Animal Barnyard; a Kid Corral play area with mazes, rope swings, and slides; plus a country store, a shady oak grove picnic area, and, of course, the ever-popular train ride. It is not unusual to see as many as two thousand folks enjoying the outdoors over the Memorial Day weekend.

PHOTO BY ALAN S. WEINER

PHOTO BY DAVE GALEN

A Company on the Move

We speak our customers' language

American Home Mortgage (AHM) is a company on the move. In early 2006 it was ranked by *Forbes* magazine, for the second year running, among the top two thousand public companies in the world—up two hundred places from the previous year. AHM offers residential mortgage loan products for first-time, move-up, and investment home buyers. The Ashburn, Virginia, office provides same-day preapprovals, and clients can choose to make loan application by phone, online, or in person.

"With more than two thousand loan products available, we make sure to fully understand a client's financing needs and goals before recommending a program," said AHM area manager Maryam McDaniel, "and we take time to explain our products in familiar terms. It's just our way of doing business and giving back to the community. Our loan officers represent a world market."

In fact, while diversity may be a buzzword to many, at the Ashburn branch it is a reality. Since opening the office in 2004 McDaniel has recruited a knowledgeable staff representing a variety of cultural backgrounds, ages, and lifestyles. The combined staff speaks a total of seven languages: Farsi, Punjabi, Hindi, Urdu, German, Spanish, and English.

McDaniel explains, "Being able to communicate with people in their native language is a great advantage. We bring to the process an understanding of different cultures."

Your local Loudoun County American Home Mortgage family, with over twenty-five years of experience.

McDaniel plans to open five or six new American Home locations in nearby communities. She also notes that, wherever they are located, the branches will quickly become known by being active in the community. The Ashburn team, for example, has supported such organizations as the Susan G. Komen Foundation, Habitat for Humanity, and the National MS Society.

The Ashburn team also works hand-in-hand with area businesses, such as the Dulles Area Association of REALTORS (DAAR) and the Loudoun County Chamber of Commerce. "In 2006, we supported DAAR's annual convention. The partnership worked so well, we've been asked to provide more training and presentations," said McDaniel.

McDaniel is big on education. She works with counselors in the Loudoun County Public Schools to help prepare students for life after high school, arranging internships and working in classrooms to teach teens about credit and how to use it wisely.

"In addition to helping people move into homes, we also provide them with solutions to manage and restructure their finances to better help them reach their financial goals. Assisting people is definitely the best part of my job," she said.

Customers certainly appreciate the personal attention they get from McDaniel's team, as evidenced by American Home Mortgage's rate of growth in Loudoun County.

American Home Mortgage is an equal housing lender, licensed or authorized in the fifty states and the District of Columbia. ◆

"Being able to communicate with people in their native language is a great advantage. We bring to the process an understanding of different cultures."

Area manager Maryam McDaniel of American Home Mortgage, attending the settlement with her clients till the very end to ensure that the loan process goes smoothly.

PHOTO BY DAVE GALEN

PHOTO BY ALAN S. WEINER

With more than twenty years of real estate settlement experience and several licensed title agents, F & M Title's processing staff has the knowledge and capacity to handle most real estate issues. Their settlement agents take great pride in walking clients through the process very carefully, which allows the customers to leave the table with a strong sense of confidence.

America ... The Land of Opportunity

As a home buyer, you have a choice

One of the major advantages of shopping in America is the number of choices we have. However, many home buyers do not realize they have a choice of settlement companies.

"Generally the Realtor or mortgage broker will guide buyers toward a specific title company. We want folks to know that when the purchase contracts are being written, they should ask for good-faith estimates from several settlement companies. Buyers may be surprised that fees and quality of service can vary greatly," said Chip Oswalt, executive vice president of F & M Title & Escrow.

Another benefit of dealing with a personalized company like F & M is that they will work with a Realtor or a mortgage broker to negotiate closing costs and pass those savings along to the buyer.

At the moment, F & M Title deals mostly with professional-based customers such as Realtors and mortgage bankers. However, plans are in place to begin an education program aimed at first-time buyers or homeowners planning to refinance. "Targeting the end user will enable us to educate our customers as well as to serve them better," said Oswalt.

With major purchases, the bottom line is all important, and the bottom line at F & M Title is as follows: "We assure our customers of a complete legally binding process that gives them the insurance they need at fair and reasonable prices," said Mack McDaniel, president and founder of F&M Title. ✦

"Targeting the end user will enable us to educate our customers as well as to serve them better."

Businesses, schools, universities, and community partnerships all play a part in Loudoun's growing emphasis on life sciences. The opening of the $500 million Howard Hughes Medical Institute's Janelia Farm Research Campus, where many of the world's leading scientists are pursuing long-term research in an environment designed to bring together researchers from disparate disciplines, has brought international attention to Loudoun's life sciences market. Loudoun's educational resources, such as the Loudoun Academy of Science and the nation's first undergraduate degree program in pharmacogenomics at George Washington University, are developing our brightest students into the next generation of life science leaders. Loudoun has also helped foster collaboration among the life sciences community through such innovative activities as the Science and Technology Cabinet and sponsorship of the Medical Automation and Mid-Atlantic Bio Conferences. Below, Science and Technology Cabinet Chair Leslie Platt, County Science Advisor Terry Sharrer, and Loudoun Academy of Science Director George Wolfe oversee student research.

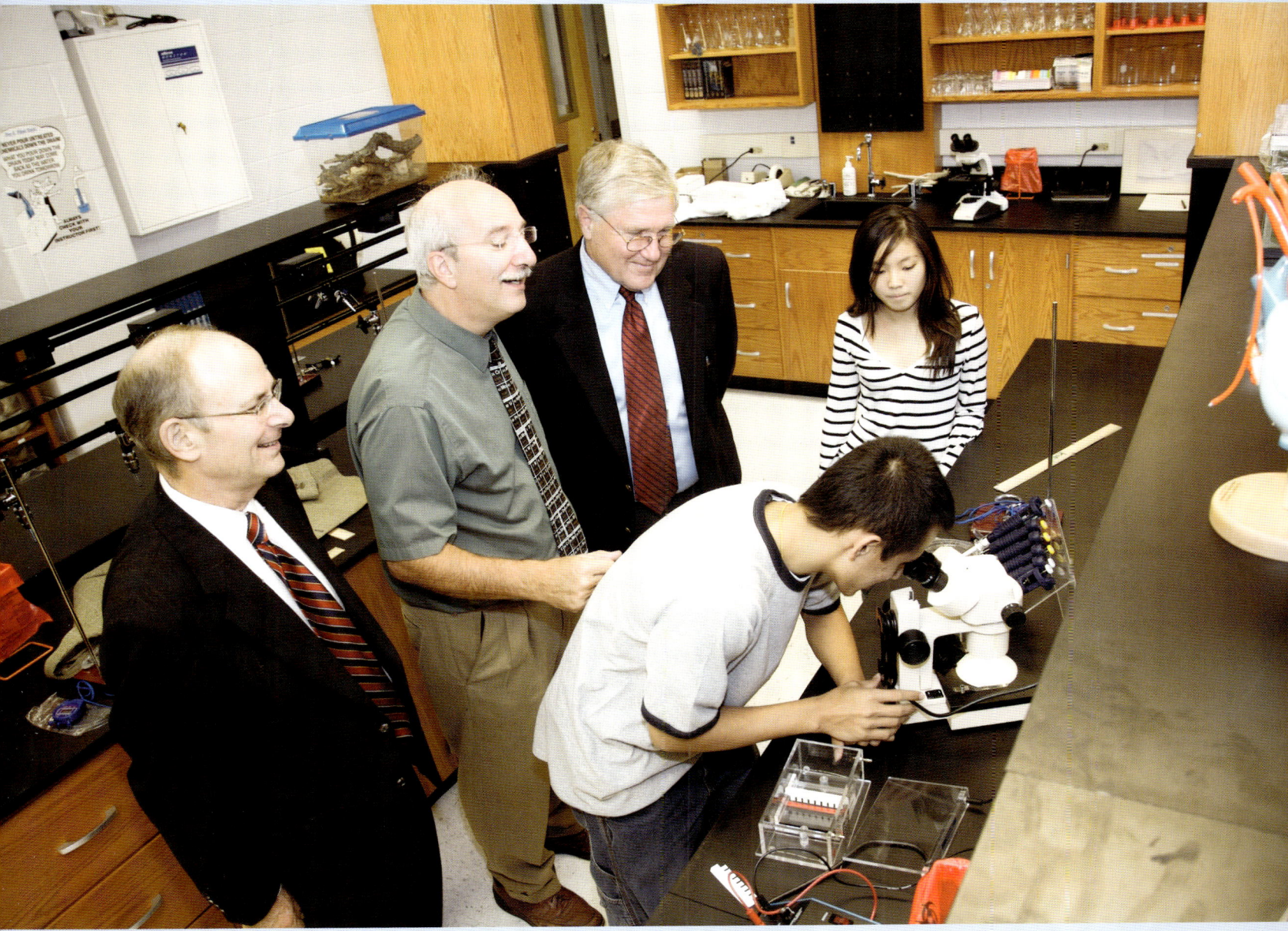

PHOTO BY JEANETTE BURKLE

The Fourth of July Celebration in Historic Downtown Leesburg is a classic community celebration. Families, neighbors, and friends gather to watch the parade during the day, and fireworks at Ida Lee in the evening.

PHOTO BY JEANETTE BURKLE

PHOTO BY JEANETTE BURKLE

PHOTO BY JEANETTE BURKLE

PHOTO BY ALAN S. WEINER

Education…Dividends for a Lifetime

Preparing well-rounded students for the leadership of tomorrow

Notre Dame Academy is a Catholic coeducational college preparatory high school that accepts day students from all denominations. Notre Dame Academy develops young men and women of character and moral integrity who will emerge as responsible leaders in a diverse and ever-changing world.

"Notre Dame Academy develops students in the pursuit of lifelong learning, service to others, spiritual growth, and the success of each student," says Headmaster John Borley. "We believe in the development of the whole person in mind, body, and spirit. Consequently, our students can handle anything they encounter in college and later in the pursuit of their careers and families." With a 100 percent college matriculation rate, this philosophy of well-rounded preparation is essential, as college acceptance is a requirement for graduation. To support each student, the school provides a number of ways to assist students with organizational and learning skills. Parent Cathy Struder puts it another way: "The way many graduates describe the support and attention they receive is that not only are they prepared academically when they go to college, they are happy with who they are as people, and confident that they will succeed."

Notre Dame Academy's self-imposed limit of three hundred students drives the school's ability to deliver an environment of both individual and collective discovery, exploration, challenge, and achievement. "Small class sizes, a dedicated and experienced faculty and staff, and a spiritual culture guided by compassion, respect, and tolerance provide the foundation for the success of each student," says Borley. In addition, there are myriad opportunities for student participation in extracurricular activities such as athletics and arts, as well as community service. As a result, there is something to interest nearly every student, and the participation rate is extremely high. The importance of extracurricular activities is clear; when young adults are free to explore and make decisions, they often develop interests for life, as well as a better understanding of the decision-making process.

In addition to nurturing well-rounded students, Notre Dame Academy produces top-level graduates who are highly sought by colleges and universities. Every student at Notre Dame Academy must complete thirty-two credits to graduate—twenty-eight of which are academic credits, and four are theological studies. "The curriculum is structured for the highest experience, and includes honors, Advanced Placement, and college-credit courses," explains Arnold Klingenberg, assistant headmaster for academics. "Our requirements for math, science, and language guarantee our students a thorough look by colleges and universities." Clearly, a Notre Dame Academy education pays dividends for a lifetime. ◆

"We believe in the development of the whole person in mind, body, and spirit."

Notre Dame Academy is known for its open and inviting environment, where diversity is embraced, and respect for self, for one another, and for community is a priority.

Notre Dame Academy lacrosse team in action. The school has an exceptionally high participation rate in athletics and other extracurricular activities.

PHOTO BY ALAN S. WEINER

The Squirts, the age group for players ten and under, are part of the Ashburn Inline Hockey League (AIHL). This is an official USA Hockey Inline–sanctioned league, and it has the largest membership in northern Virginia. The league is about having fun and learning to play organized hockey. It also provides a place for the youth of Ashburn, Sterling, and surrounding areas to learn the fundamentals in a safe environment. AIHL has league play in six divisions for ages from four to seventeen. There are two playing seasons, fall and spring. Each season consists of ten games plus the playoffs, which bring out a lot of good-natured competition. As the league officials are quick to point out, having a good time and learning the game are equally as important as winning. All the games are played at the Dulles Sportsplex rink. So what does it take to get into the playoffs? In a word, practice, practice, practice, although coaches try to hold it to one evening a week.

PHOTO BY SCOTT INDERMAUR

Through a partnership with the Transitions Team, an organization that is dedicated to building a bridge between high school and independent living, Nova Medical Group has provided jobs for students with varying abilities, internships, discounts toward student physicals, discounts for teachers at the medical spa, and much more. It is just one way the Nova team reaches out to the community it calls home. Here, Shirley Grimmet, transition teacher at Briar Woods High School; Melissa Hartman, the transition and special education supervisor for Loudoun County Schools; and Michele Havener, the assistant principal at Briar Woods High School gather with students from the Briar Woods science department as Nova donates lab coats to the school. (L–R) Arash Hamidi, Jennifer Potts, Jeffrey S. Horvath, Michele Havener, Donna Armani, Christina Downs, Grace Keenan, MD, Melissa Hartman, Shirley Grimmet, Charlie Pierce, and Shetal Patel.

The names may vary from place to place, but the intent of Take Your Kids to Work Day is the same everywhere. Throughout the United States and Canada millions of young people see where their parents work, achieve some insight into what they do, and are exposed to a wide variety of job and career options. Whether working on a makeshift assembly line, developing a mock sales presentation, or finding out what providing customer service is all about, it usually turns out to be a day of discovery for everyone, parents and children alike. Employees' children at NEW, a company that provides extended service contracts and buyer protection programs for consumer products, pulled the curtain back on the corporate world, and at the end of the day, the children picked up a paycheck. Not bad for the first day on a new job.

Caregiving…It's a Team Effort

One group providing you infinite possibilities

As northern Virginia's largest physician-owned multispecialty medical provider and one of the leading employers and community service participants, Loudoun Medical Group is a testament to the power of teamwork and commitment.

The organization was formed in June 2000 by a group of physicians from a variety of specialties. Each had been independently providing high-quality medical care in the area for years, but by joining forces, they could offer even greater benefits to their patients. Improved operational efficiency was achieved by working collectively through a centralized administrative office; now doctors and nurses could concentrate the majority of their efforts on patient care.

"That we are a physician-owned, -governed, and -directed organization is key," says CEO Jim Lapsley. "Physician-directed medical groups are highly successful because they are directly involved with patients and day-to-day operations. Our number-one priority is to support the Loudoun community by ensuring an ongoing quality of care."

Located in one of the fastest-growing regions in the country, LMG has distinguished itself in a wide range of medical specialties, including pediatrics, family medicine, obstetrics and gynecology, general surgery, urgent care, orthopedic surgery, integrative medicine, radiation oncology, and occupational medicine, to name just a few.

"In our ongoing commitment to providing the region with a range of specialties, we are continually examining our communities' needs and bringing in new physicians to accommodate those needs," continues Lapsley.

PHOTO BY SCOTT INDERMAUR

A Loudoun Medical Group nurse gives expert care to a patient in the group's Immediate Care Center located at 46440 Benedict Drive, Suite 107, Sterling, Virginia. The LMG Immediate Care Center has been open since August 2005, when the group's leadership recognized a lack of options for nonemergency urgent medical care in Loudoun County. Since then, the LMG ICC has provided high-quality care to thousands of patients in an attractive setting with minimal wait time.

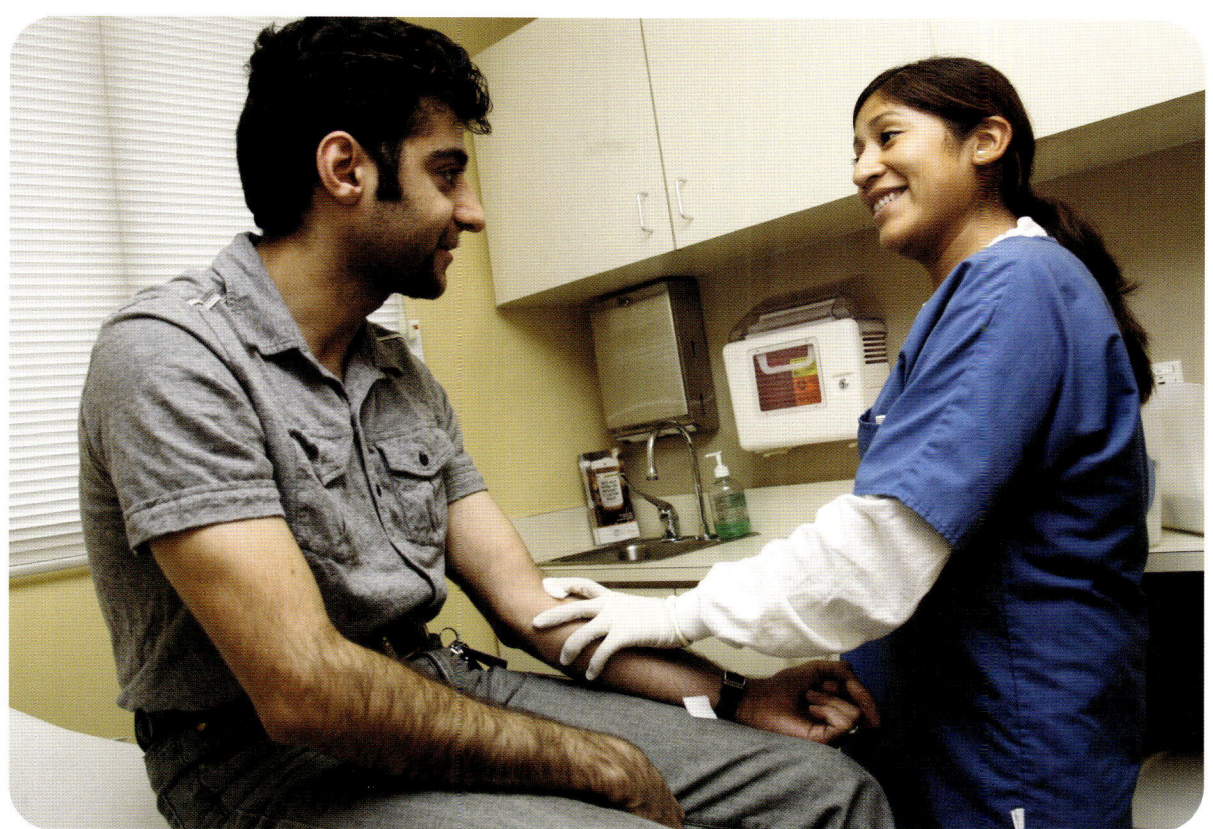

PHOTO BY DAVE GALEN

Loudoun Medical Group is one of the region's leading employers, with over 480 employees who perform a variety of functions, from physicians and clinical staff to administrators and information technology experts. LMG's commitment to being a leading employer is seen through the group's employee-focused programs, including groupwide orientation and training programs and an employee wellness program.

Forging collaborative relationships outside the group is also critical to LMG's success, he says. "We want to continue to be a resource and partner and establish relationships with insurance companies, hospitals, and other health-care providers to provide the best, most efficient health-care services to the citizens of Loudoun County."

That also means streamlining the administrative and record-keeping process. To reduce check-in times, LMG's Web site provides an easy-to-use doctor locator service as well as downloadable New Patient Registration and HIPAA Notice forms. In addition, Loudoun Medical Group is in the process of implementing an Electronic Medical Record (EMR) system, which allows real-time updating of patient information so that diagnoses, lab results, allergies, medications, and immunization records are easily accessed at the touch of a screen. Laboratory test results are now directly fed into patients' charts for provider verification and better continuity of care, including an increase in availability of shared patient information between other providers and practices.

Headquartered in Leesburg, LMG currently serves over eight hundred thousand patients a year at thirty-three sites located throughout Loudoun and Fairfax counties. With over 480 professionals and support staff, LMG is also one of the largest employers in the region, and is currently ranked number twenty-four in Loudoun County.

continued on page 82

"Our number-one priority is to support the Loudoun community by ensuring an ongoing quality of care."

East Garden
Concept Landscape Study

An architect's rendering of the Cornwall Medical Pavilion, future home to many Loudoun Medical Group offices. The Cornwall Medical Pavilion will be a one-hundred-thousand-square-foot medical office building constructed on Loudoun Hospital's Leesburg campus and will feature the latest developments in medical technology to offer patients compassionate and innovative care modalities.

continued from page 81

Loudoun Medical Group takes that ranking seriously. "We're committed to being a responsible employer," says Lapsley. "So we are always looking for new and innovative employee benefits and incentives, with a focus on employee morale, retention, and ongoing training."

In addition to competitive benefit and salary packages, employees can take advantage of such innovative programs as LMG's Employee Wellness Program. Begun in July 2006, the ten-week, ten-class program includes both a healthy living as well as weight loss component. Classes cover a range of topics including proper nutrition, healthy exercise, stress management and relaxation, healthy cooking demonstrations, and personal motivation. The program is free to participating employees and also includes discounted rates to several local health clubs.

Embracing its physicians' long-standing commitment to their communities at large, the Loudoun Medical Group Charitable Foundation is actively involved in numerous initiatives throughout the region and even the nation.

Jim Lapsley, CEO of Loudoun Medical Group, along with Dr. Martha Calihan, medical director and Dr. Bruce Thomas, LMG board chairman, receive Inova Healthcare System's 2006 Commitment to Excellence Award for Community Responsibility for LMG's free clinic in Bay St. Louis, Mississippi, from Inova CEO Knox Singleton (left).

Many of the most recognizable faces in Loudoun County's medical community, the shareholders of Loudoun Medical Group (the largest physician-owned multispecialty medical group in Virginia), are active community leaders and some of the most highly respected physicians in Loudoun.

PHOTO BY DAVE GALEN

When Hurricane Katrina devastated the Gulf Coast, the foundation organized a series of community fund-raisers that allowed LMG to establish, fund, and operate a free medical clinic in Bay St. Louis, Mississippi, which was completely devastated by the hurricane. Thanks to LMG's direction and the generosity of dozens of local individuals and businesses, the clinic provided ten months of free care to over eighteen thousand individuals. And during the holidays, LMG once again rallied the local community in a holiday gift drive that brought the spirit of the season to hundreds of Bay St. Louis families.

Demonstrating the power of like-minded individuals working together, LMG's approach to care starts with the patient and extends outward. Says Lapsley of their focus: "We're one group with infinite possibilities." ✦

Jim Lapsley, CEO, and Martha Calihan, MD, medical director, review construction progress on a new Loudoun Medical Group office. Loudoun Medical Group's growth and development throughout Loudoun County, particularly in Western Loudoun, help residents receive the best-quality health care possible.

PHOTO BY DAVE GALEN

Loudoun County celebrates its 250th anniversary in 2007. While much has changed in two-and-a-half centuries, in many ways the heart of the community remains the same. Blossoming eighteenth-century Loudoun received new residents of German, Scottish, and Irish descent from neighboring states, just as today the county welcomes thousands of residents annually from the region and the world. Nineteenth-century Loudoun developed into an agrarian society centered around distinct towns, just as thriving contemporary suburban developments and historic towns today provide contrast to 160,000 acres of rural landscape. As seen in these two photos taken more than one hundred years apart (near the village of Aldie around 1900, and at the Lincoln School in 2006), perhaps the most common and enduring value in Loudoun is the importance placed on our children, who throughout our history have represented the very best of the county's future.

PHOTO COURTESY OF THOMAS BALCH LIBRARY

PHOTO BY VICKIE BELLEROSE

Getting out into the community allows the team at Nova Medical Group to help local residents of all ages understand how important it is to maximize their wellness by understanding their bodies and taking care of themselves. Here, Carol Coloma, FNP, checks the blood pressure of a Senior Health Fair attendee, one of the many people who benefited from Nova's visit to the event.

On a Mission

Helping you find the perfect place to call home

Every other month, real estate agent Sherry Wilson hosts a party at her home. The guest list always comprises nearly one hundred new and longtime clients, who have the chance to mix and mingle with their Loudoun County neighbors. The event fosters a genuine sense of community and goodwill for everyone in attendance, and it's a particularly important function for Sherry, as helping people find that feeling of home and belonging has been a primary goal for this successful RE/MAX professional since she began her real estate career in 1984.

Formerly a full-time teacher at Simpson Middle School in Leesburg, Wilson decided to pursue real estate as a side business in the early 1980s. With her extensive knowledge of Loudoun County, she believed she could find fulfillment by assisting just one or two people a year with their home buying and selling needs. She never expected to become one of the county's and country's most prolific agents. Sherry explains, "Every time I helped someone find the perfect property or sell the home they were in, it was magical for me. It was the same magic feeling I got when I knew I had helped the children grasp a new concept or idea. I just love that feeling."

PHOTO BY THOMAS S. ENGLAND

A Loudoun County Transit Bus brings to the public the message of "Sherry's Team Assures Your Success." It's just one of the creative ways the team lets community residents know that every member is there to help with all of their real estate needs.

PHOTO BY JEANETTE BURKLE

In the first year after securing her license, Sherry was named Rookie of the Year; the following year, she was Loudoun County's top-producing agent. Remarkably, she reached these heights while continuing her career in education. By the late 1980s, though, she made the leap to full-time agent, and today she operates a RE/MAX office with twenty-six team members, including agents and administrative staff. Since 1999, Sherry Wilson & Co. has earned the distinction each year of being the number-one RE/MAX Agent/ Team in Virginia and in the Central Atlantic Region, as well as the number-two, -three, or -four RE/MAX Agent/Team in the United States and Across the World since 2000.

"I'm very thankful that I have wonderful team members," Wilson observes. "I've always been able to count on the people around me, and I could not do it without them."

While Sherry attributes her team's success to the people she works with, she also believes that their collective mission of building long-lasting relationships, providing services beyond people's expectations, and adhering to core values like excellence, honesty, and integrity have contributed to the group's accomplishments. Furthermore, not only does the team concept afford clients consistent attention and support, but also access to comprehensive resources, from experienced marketing professionals to a dedicated courier service. "We want to be our clients' Realtor, but we also want to be their expert when they need something," Sherry notes.

As a longtime resident of Loudoun County, Wilson not only has been able to share her comprehensive knowledge about the local market with her clients, but also with the members of her team, including the professional listing agents pictured here. With access to that kind of wisdom, it's no wonder that everyone who is a part of Sherry Wilson & Co. has found great success.

"We're always trying to improve . . . so that our clients are served better than they can be served anywhere else."

continued on page 88

PHOTO BY BRUCE R. FEELEY

Here, Sherry Wilson proudly stands in front of her Purcellville office, which has been home to RE/MAX Leaders Sherry Wilson & Co. since 1999. From this location, twenty-six dedicated real estate professionals work diligently every day to provide clients with the kind of award-winning customer service that has become synonymous with the enthusiastic team.

continued from page 87

From helping them pinpoint the right financial institution for their needs to offering them the chance to use Sherry Wilson & Co.'s two moving trucks, Sherry's team ensures that every client has the best real estate experience possible from beginning to end.

These days, Sherry Wilson travels the country sharing her expertise with rising real estate professionals, teaching at such seminars as Howard Brinton's STAR POWER Systems. She and her team also spend time giving back to the community through numerous charitable efforts, like sponsoring local sports teams and working with the Children's Miracle Network. And they show the same dedication to those activities as they do to staying on the cutting edge of the real estate industry. Sherry concludes, "We're always trying to improve our systems and improve in technology—trying to get the best all the time so that our clients are served better than they can be served anywhere else." ✦

Sherry and her team enjoy entertaining her clients at her highly anticipated annual Margaritaville dinner party, which includes a band, tethered balloon rides, fun for the children, and much more.

This middle school and Environmental Educational Center are part of the overall plan created by Greenvest, which is a residential builder of planned communities. The four distinct communities under way will bring world-class amenities to Loudoun County, while providing a place for generations of Loudoun's future families to live, work, and grow.

The statue erected at George Mason University's North Plaza serves as both a symbol of what the school stands for and as a good-luck charm for the student body. Commissioned by the George Mason Fund for the Arts and the Arts Gala Committee, and sculpted by acclaimed artist Wendy M. Ross, the seven-foot-high statue was dedicated on April 12, 1996. It depicts the American statesman, civil rights champion, and Virginia native presenting his handwritten first draft of the Virginia Declaration of Rights to the fifth Virginia Convention of Delegates. It was during this convention, held in Williamsburg in May, June, and July 1776, that Virginia declared its independence from Britain. During school sports activities and other events, it's become a tradition for various student and faculty groups to vie for the right to decorate George as a way to increase school spirit. Rubbing his toe before an exam is also considered good luck

Answering Growing Call for Research

Meeting the area's technology and telecommunications demands

Testing the durability of the bollards installed around embassies and government buildings domestically and abroad to protect them from terrorist acts is an example of the diverse research projects undertaken by the National Crash Analysis Center (NCAC) located at the George Washington University Virginia Campus in Ashburn, Virginia. The NCAC is one of fifteen research centers, labs, and institutes now operating at the campus.

The GW Virginia Campus offers more than twenty certificate and graduate degree programs focusing on business, engineering, and education, with specialties ranging from information systems technology, to human and organizational learning, to telecommunications. A unique undergraduate program in pharmacogenomics, now in its second year, is the only one of its kind in the country. Students on GW's Virginia Campus also can earn undergraduate and graduate certificates in fields as diverse as aviation, justice information technology, wireless communications, and landscape design.

In addition to the NCAC, some of the research centers include the:

- Vehicle Modeling/Digitization Lab, a high-performance computing lab where safety experts run vehicle and roadside hardware crash simulations.
- Center for Intelligent Systems Research, which conducts research in the use of intelligent systems to address transportation issues such as drowsy driving in addition to investigating advanced vehicle control systems and railroad routing optimization.

- Institute for Magnetics Research, which studies unexpected behaviors of and possible practical applications for magnetic nanostructures.

- Center for Infrastructure Safety and Reliability, which conducts analytical and experimental research directed toward improving the safety and reliability of complex infrastructure and structural systems. The center houses one of only two shake table labs on the East Coast, and the largest six-degrees-of-freedom shake table in the United States.

- Integrated Justice Information Systems (IJIS) Institute, a non-profit corporation comprising approximately 160 corporate technology members involved in developing and implementing justice information systems. IJIS helped develop the computer technology and standards for the National Sex Offender Public Registry, refined the Global Justice XML Data Model (GJXDM), created the guidelines and standards to direct states in the development of Statewide Automated Victim Information and Notification (SAVIN) systems, and developed a prescription drug monitoring program information exchange to assist states in exchanging law enforcement information related to prescription drug fraud.

Anchored in the heart of University Center on Route 7—the region's technology corridor—the GW Virginia Campus opened its doors in 1991. From the university's initial $26 million investment with one building on a fifty-acre site, the Virginia Campus now occupies three buildings over ninety-five acres, with more buildings planned.

The 185-year-old George Washington University in Washington, D.C., continues investing in Loudoun County with an even greater commitment—to support the county and the region as GW continues to participate in state-of-the-art research, corporate partnerships, and advanced programming to meet regional workforce needs. ✦

More than twenty certificate and graduate degree programs are offered in education, business, and engineering.

A unique undergraduate program in pharmacogenomics is the only one of its kind in the country.

The ninety-five-acre GW Virginia Campus now boasts three buildings: a research building (the original building), an administration building, and a third building on permanent lease to the National Transportation Safety Board (NTSB) Academy.

In 1943, Waterford residents established the Waterford Foundation to preserve and protect their town's eighteenth- and nineteenth-century architecture. That same year, the founders also held their first fund-raiser. Today the event has grown into a hugely popular crafts fair and homes tour that draws thousands of visitors from across the region and the country. Held for three days each October, the Waterford Homes Tour and Crafts Exhibit helps raise funds for the foundation's ongoing restoration projects, as well as its living history program, an architectural stewardship lecture series, and a concert series held in Waterford's Old School auditorium.

PHOTO BY THOMAS S. ENGLAND

PHOTO BY THOMAS S. ENGLAND

THE CORNER STORE

WATERFORD
FOUNDATION

PHOTO BY THOMAS S. ENGLAND

PHOTO BY BRUCE R. FEELEY

A Legacy of Excellence

World-class care is right around the corner

HCA has roots deeply imbedded in Virginia's soil. For nearly forty years, it has evolved to meet the changing needs of area residents, and today it includes twelve hospital campuses, five surgery centers, and three imaging centers that serve 1.2 million people each year. With facilities in northern, central, and southwestern Virginia, HCA Virginia plays a pivotal role in the well-being of the Commonwealth—improving people's lives in many different ways.

In northern Virginia, HCA's Capital Division is headquartered in Reston. From this central location, HCA Virginia manages two hospitals in northern Virginia—Dominion Hospital, a 100-bed psychiatric facility in Falls Church, and Reston Hospital Center, a 187-bed acute care hospital—as well as outpatient surgery centers in Reston and Fairfax County.

Reston Hospital Center is a full-service, acute-care hospital in western Fairfax County that serves patients from Fairfax and Loudoun counties. It was built by HCA in 1986 (replacing Circle Terrace Hospital), following a grassroots campaign by area residents who recognized the need for more health-care facilities. Opened with 127 beds, it later added 60 new beds and renovated and expanded its endoscopy, medical records, and emergency departments. This $100 million expansion also featured a new parking garage, medical office building, and outpatient surgery center.

The Family Center at Reston Hospital Center welcomes more than three thousand babies each year. The Family Center features all private rooms with traditionally elegant decor and a Level 2 Neonatal Intensive Care Unit with twenty-four-hour, in-house physician coverage.

Just eighteen miles east of Reston Hospital Center in Falls Church, HCA Virginia's Dominion Hospital is the region's only free-standing mental health hospital. With 100 inpatient beds and a wide variety of partial hospitalization programs, Dominion Hospital provides care for children, adolescents, and adults, and it specializes in crisis stabilization and treatment of acute psychiatric anxiety, depression, mood disorders, and other mental health conditions.

In response to the region's extraordinary growth and public demand for improved access to health care, HCA Virginia plans to build two new hospitals: Broadlands Regional Medical Center, a 164-bed hospital in Ashburn, and 130-bed Spotsylvania Regional Medical Center in Fredericksburg. Both of these hospitals have received Certificate of Public Need approval from the state; once operational, they will bring new jobs to the region and create more choice in the marketplace.

Aside from its role as a health-care provider, HCA Virginia has a positive impact in the Commonwealth in many other ways. As one of the state's largest employers, HCA Virginia generates thirteen thousand good-paying jobs that are a stimulus for the state's economy. And the company's tax revenues—which exceed $100 million annually—pay for vital community services, including road improvements, teacher salaries, emergency responder squads, and

HCA Virginia is committed to ensuring that all patients receive the type of high-quality care they deserve.

continued on page 98

The Women's Imaging Center at Reston Hospital Center offers mammography, ultrasound, and bone-density exams in a comfortable, spa-like environment. The center is proud to offer digital mammography, 4-D ultrasound, and computer-aided diagnostics.

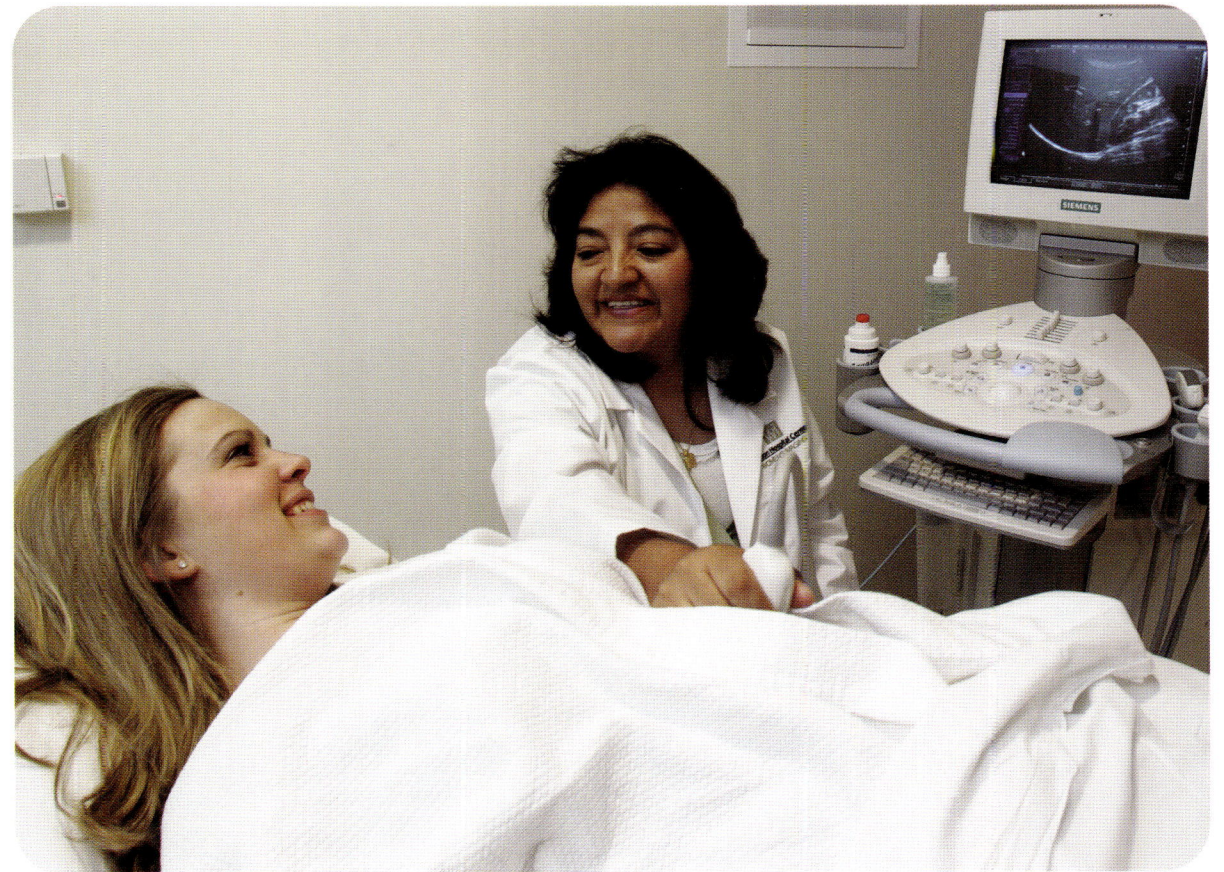

PHOTO BY ALAN S. WEINER

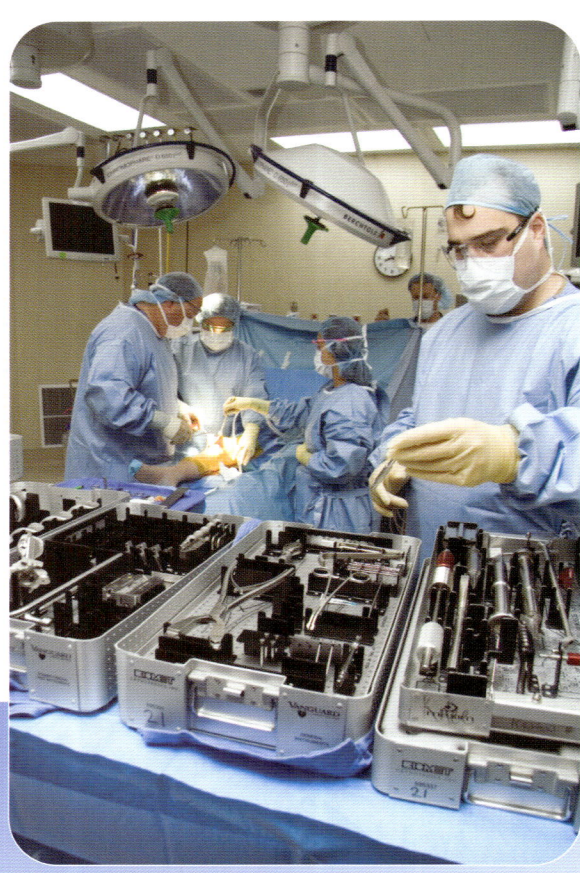

Reston Hospital Center offers both inpatient and outpatient surgery. The Surgical Services team, in cooperation with the local physician community, uses the latest in surgical technology to care for more than twelve thousand patients each year.

continued from page 97

many others. Finally, as a concerned and engaged corporate citizen, HCA Virginia seeks out opportunities to identify and address broad community needs. Each year, the organization provides more than $100 million in free care to uninsured patients

PHOTO BY BRUCE R. FEELEY

Dominion Hospital reflects HCA's commitment to patient safety and the reduction of medical errors through the eMAR & Bar Coding initiative. The system checks each medication order against the patient's medication history and assures that the correct medication is given at the correct time.

PHOTO BY BRUCE R. FEELEY

who cannot afford to pay their medical expenses. The company also donates funds and in-kind services to assist nonprofit organizations that selflessly serve the less fortunate in our communities.

HCA Virginia takes pride in touching many people in many ways, as an indispensable health-care resource, a responsive community partner, and a catalyst for economic growth in the Commonwealth. ✦

Access to high-quality health care is a vital quality-of-life issue facing Loudoun County residents today and into the future. HCA's Broadlands Regional Medical Center is a planned, state-of-the-art, acute-care hospital that will provide access to health care, as well as taxes, jobs, and stewardship for the community.

Using expressive therapies, like art or movement therapy, patients explore and gain clarity about their thoughts and feelings. Dominion Hospital offers a full range of therapies for children, adolescents, and adults receiving treatment for mental health disorders.

PHOTO BY BRUCE R. FEELEY

Colorful tulips seem to bob their heads to announce the arrival of spring and the Annual Historic Garden Week in Virginia Tour. In Loudoun County, the event is sponsored by the Fauquier-Loudoun Garden Club and the Leesburg Garden Club, two of the members of the statewide association, the Garden Club of Virginia. Lovely gardens and beautiful homes are open for tours during the ten-day April event. Since 1929, proceeds from the Annual Historic Garden Week have funded many restoration projects. In addition, the income from the tour provides two annual fellowships for landscape architecture students.

A century-old stone wall encircles Edenwald Farm like strong and protective arms. The sixty-acre farm sits atop Catocin Mountain just outside the town of Leesburg. Its residents include the Kalitkas, who moved here in 1994 to raise Blue-faced Leister sheep, angora rabbits, angora goats, and llamas—all creatures whose fur is used to spin yarns. "We're starting from what God gives us and working our way up to the finished product," says Pat Kalitka, who spins the fibers herself. "Spinning is a lot like knitting—all muscle memory. It's so Zen-like; it's wonderful." When she can, Pat uses plants on the property for natural dyes for the yarns. Angora, which comes from the angora rabbit, is an extremely warm fiber, so it is often used for socks, mufflers, scarves, and hats. "It's a lot like silk—very fine, durable, and it takes color so well," she adds.

Chapter Two

WORK!

Loudoun County has always played a crucial role in the development of Virginia's economy. In recent decades, it has also served as headquarters for some of our nation's most vital industries.

For more than two centuries, agriculture was the county's dominant economy. That began to change in the early 1960s with the construction of Dulles International Airport in the southwestern part of the county. Not only did the airport attract new businesses to the area, it established the county as a gateway to the nation's capital.

As a result, Loudoun County has grown into one of the most dynamic regions in the country. With a population of a quarter of a million residents, Loudoun also serves a regional market of over 5 million people—an employment base that is currently among the strongest in the nation in terms of purchasing power and job skills.

For the past several decades, Loudoun has experienced a boom in high-tech businesses. Companies such as Verizon, America Online, and M. C. Dean benefit from Loudoun's strong commitment to higher education, its diverse business environment, and its proximity to Washington, D.C. Not only does it serve as headquarters for some of the world's most successful technology-based industries, Loudoun County also provides the employment base necessary to ensure the continued success of homegrown enterprises like Bridgman Communications and the Miles LeHane Group.

Small businesses also thrive here. Loudoun's numerous towns and villages provide unique opportunities for businesses that cater to tourism—everything from boutiques and art galleries to restaurants and bed and breakfasts. And while many entrepreneurial start-ups and professional services choose to locate to the county's office and industrial parks, Loudoun's small towns also have their advantages, including a slower pace once outside the office.

Loudoun retains a strong rural economy in its western section. Here, the equine industry reigns, bringing in an estimated $78 million a year to the state's economy. Other booming rural-based businesses include nearly a dozen local wineries and over twenty-five farms and nurseries.

With its pro-business environment and advantageous location, it's no wonder that hundreds of new businesses each year decide to make Loudoun County their home base.

When former magazine editor, photographer, and writer Richard Busch first started making pottery in the 1980s, he did so simply as a hobby. But then the hobby became an obsession. "I just loved getting my hands in moist clay, making vases and bowls and other forms, learning to glaze and fire, and seeing the finished pieces come out of the kiln," he says. "It's also about the aesthetics—making something that's beautiful as well as functional." Then, in 1998, Busch retired with his wife to a twenty-acre former dairy farm outside Leesburg and was able to turn his hobby into a career. Named Glenfiddich after the Celtic word for "valley of the deer," which are frequent wild denizens of the area, the farm serves as Busch's home, workshop, and studio. Easily recognizable for their deer symbol stamp, Busch's works reflect his longtime interest in Asian design, and are created in part through the intricate process of salt firing, which yields the kind of "unpredictable results" that Busch enjoys as part of the act of creation.

From her studio in rural Loudoun County, Marilee Peterson guides the artisans of Rabbit Run Workshops. The group designs and crafts custom glass windows and doors that appeal to homeowners and builders alike. The artists work closely with clients to create pieces that perfectly suit individual tastes. Whether stained or leaded glass, Rabbit Run artists know how to use glass to bring to life the energy of any space. The workshop also designs and builds three-dimensional art pieces to suit that special space in any home or office.

Thomas Blau, laboratory technician, works with Dr. Alessandra Barelli, department manager, chemistry, to measure the impact resistance of a plastic specimen using a pendulum impact tester. The results of this test allow the chemists to refine their polymer formulations for real-world performance.

PHOTO BY ALAN S. WEINER

Unlimited Polymer Solutions

Products that optimize performance in construction, automotive, and industry

Since its founding in Rehau, Germany, in 1948, REHAU has grown from a three-man production team into a worldwide leader in the manufacture of polymer-based systems.

Today, over fourteen thousand employees on six continents ensure the ongoing success of this privately held company. The company's North American operations are guided by Dr. Kathleen Saylor, chief executive officer, from their Leesburg headquarters, which oversees more than two dozen sales offices, manufacturing plants, and technical and distribution centers.

REHAU solutions are designed for construction, automotive, and industry. In construction, REHAU engineers products that add comfort, reduce energy costs, and create healthy and safe environments. For automotive manufacturers, REHAU develops systems such as polymer bumpers that optimize design and enhance comfort and safety. And for industries ranging from furniture to appliances to transportation, REHAU provides seamlessly integrating performance and design solutions.

One reason for REHAU's stellar reputation is its real desire to help customers succeed.

One reason for REHAU's stellar reputation is its real desire to help customers succeed. Customer support, which includes training through the REHAU Academy, ensures customers are satisfied and growing in market position. A passion for the unlimited potential of polymers drives the company's ongoing quest for new solutions, which, in the construction sector, include consumer products such as heating, plumbing, fire protection, and windows.

Internally, the REHAU culture is one of diversity and professional growth that stems from a belief in lifelong learning and internal advancement. It is an environment that fosters loyalty and keeps REHAU at the forefront of polymer-based solutions. ✦

Betty Korte is no ordinary math teacher. And her "white board" is no ordinary teaching tool. Named Loudoun County's Teacher of the Year for 2006, Betty automatically became the county's representative for the *Washington Post*'s Agnes Meyer Outstanding Teacher Award for 2006—an honor that brought professional recognition and a stipend. True to the style that her colleagues at Stone Bridge High School say defines her, Betty parlayed her stipend and matching funds from her husband's company into something for the greater good: software-driven Smart Boards for the math department. "There are always the abstract-thinking kids who understand math. But there are many others who have trouble bridging the concrete and the abstract. Smart Board helps do just that. You are the mouse. You can write on the board, and the software allows you to bring all different kinds of elements into the lesson that the students can see. I compare it to making the classroom a laboratory," she says. Making concepts understandable is what this former quality-control expert for a major car manufacturer believes is her most important role as a teacher. "I feel I can explain things in a way that other people can understand them. In math particularly, a lot of people don't have confidence in themselves. I like the feeling of connection with others, of building that confidence."

Don't forget the ever popular $(x^3 + y^3)$ and $(x^3 - y^3)$. Look them up if you don't remember!!

Find all trig functions if possible:

1. $\cos(\frac{\pi}{2} - \theta) = \frac{3}{5}$ and $0 \le \theta \le \frac{\pi}{2}$.

2. $\tan x = \frac{\sqrt{3}}{3}$, $\cos x = -\frac{\sqrt{3}}{2}$

Simplify using the trig identities.

3. $\tan \theta \csc \theta$

4. $\sec^2 x(1 - si$

6. $\tan^4 x + 2\tan^2 x + 1$

7. $\csc^3 x - c$

PHOTO BY ALAN S. WEINER

Welcome
to the Historic Village of
ALDIE
Est. 1810

Listed on the National Register of Historic Places, the Aldie Mill, built in 1807, is one of the nation's oldest water-powered mills still in operation. Situated on the Little River, the mill is powered by an overshot wheel, which rotates by the force of water falling from blade to blade. The mill is a part of the Aldie Mill Historic District, located along Route 50, where visitors can also enjoy seasonal tours of the Federal-style residence of military officer and statesman Charles Fenton Mercer, a miller's house, and a stone bridge. The town's name, Aldie, was coined by Mercer in honor of his ancestral home in Scotland, Aldie Castle. Owned and operated by the Douglas family for six generations, the mill has recently been restored to working order. The unincorporated village, circa 1810, includes the Aldie Peddler Shoppes, which feature a wide range of collectibles, antiques, and home decor items as well as wines from around the world. The Aldie Peddler is also renowned for its selection of long-lasting, poly-lumber lawn furniture that is handcrafted in Amish style without the use of electricity.

PHOTO BY DAVE GALEN

National Advantage . . . Hometown Access

Combining international expertise with hands-on client service

When businesses in northern Virginia require a premier legal team to handle the complexities of business law, intellectual property issues (patent, trademark, and copyright), and commercial litigation, they turn to Dunlap, Grubb & Weaver to make sense of it all and to protect their interests. And in so doing, they gain the experience of this highly touted boutique firm found right in their own backyard, named one of twelve Top Northern Virginia Law Firms by *Northern Virginia* magazine (July 2006).

"Like so many businesses in Loudoun County, we're headquartered here in Leesburg, but we're servicing clients locally, nationally, and in many cases, internationally," says partner Thomas Dunlap, former president of the Loudoun County Bar Association (2005–2006). "Our advantage is that we also have offices just blocks from the U.S. Patent and Trademark Office in Alexandria and the copyright office in D.C. While we're able to service clients well with that kind of national advantage, our local clients get that benefit also," he says. Client John Wimbrough of Shared Flight, LLC, a unique Leesburg-based aircraft company, agrees. "I'm stunned to find such high talent in Leesburg. I wanted a firm to be right here in my hometown, where I live, and where my business is going to be," says Wimbrough.

Another reason clients hire Dunlap, Grubb & Weaver is to tap into the firm's expertise in corporate law, particularly as it relates to business start-ups and acquisitions. For example, Shared Flight is the only fractional aircraft business in Loudoun; the company acquires aircrafts for owners who want to own a fraction of the aircraft for their own personal use. While Wimbrough knew he would be successful filling a market demand, he was unfamiliar with the industry. "I had no idea how to start this, as I'd never been in the airplane business myself," he says. "The fact that Jeff Weaver has an MBA with real-world experience meant that he understood the business direction I was attempting. They set it up perfectly."

Clients of Dunlap, Grubb & Weaver are also impressed with the firm's responsiveness—the heart of client service, according to partner Jeffrey Weaver. "We're keenly aware of time expenditures and the need for efficiency, so we try to provide the most cost-beneficial mix of experience, hourly rates, and availability to meet the client's needs. As a result, our clients generally feel that the work we perform is an extremely good value for their money, and they appreciate our efforts to meet their needs on their schedule," Weaver explains. In every case, one partner is always hands-on. For client Paul Hester, entrepreneur and founder of Rapid Reality, a successful video game development company headquartered in Atlanta, Georgia, having access to a partner 24/7 is critical. "Communication and continuity are the essence of what I'm trying to do. I'm paying the law firm for the principals' knowledge, education, and experience," says Hester. "You can find an attorney anywhere; finding the attorney that understands what you're doing is essential." And when that legal authority and expertise is right here in Leesburg, that's not just icing on the proverbial cake. That's a key ingredient. ✦

(From left) Grubb, Weaver, and Dunlap, pictured here in front of the Loudoun County Courthouse, represent clients in local, national, and international business transactions and litigation matters.

"You can find an attorney anywhere; finding the attorney that understands what you're doing is essential."

Weaver and Dunlap enjoy an on-site visit to client Shared Flight's headquarters at Leesburg Executive Airport. Shared Flight is Loudoun's only corporate fractional aircraft ownership program.

PHOTO BY ALAN S. WEINER

"One lawyer in the family is enough." With those words, spoken back in 1914, Jesse Nichols sealed the fate of his son Edward Enoch Nichols. Rather than becoming a lawyer, Edward opened Nichols Hardware with his partner Paul Ambrose Warner. The store located on North Twenty-first Street has been operated by the same family ever since, making it the oldest retail store of its kind in the Virginia Piedmont. Back in the days of party lines, and a central telephone exchange operator, Nichols's newspaper ads read, "Call Central, and Say 'Nichols & Warner, Please.' That's us. We have the largest and most complete stock of hardware and furniture in the county. Prices Right." Ken Nichols and his nephew Ted, who operate the store today, will tell you that although Central is long gone, the description of the stock is still accurate. Walls are lined with storage drawers containing almost any- and everything a person might need. Back in the '20s, Nichols added a picture framing business in the basement. Today Nichols is one of the few hardware stores in the area that screen frames and repair screening. It addition the store sharpens knives and shears, repairs lamps and electrical fixtures, and cuts and threads steel pipe. The one thing Nichols does not have is a computer. Every customer walks away with a handwritten receipt for each purchase.

PHOTO BY THOMAS S. ENGLAND

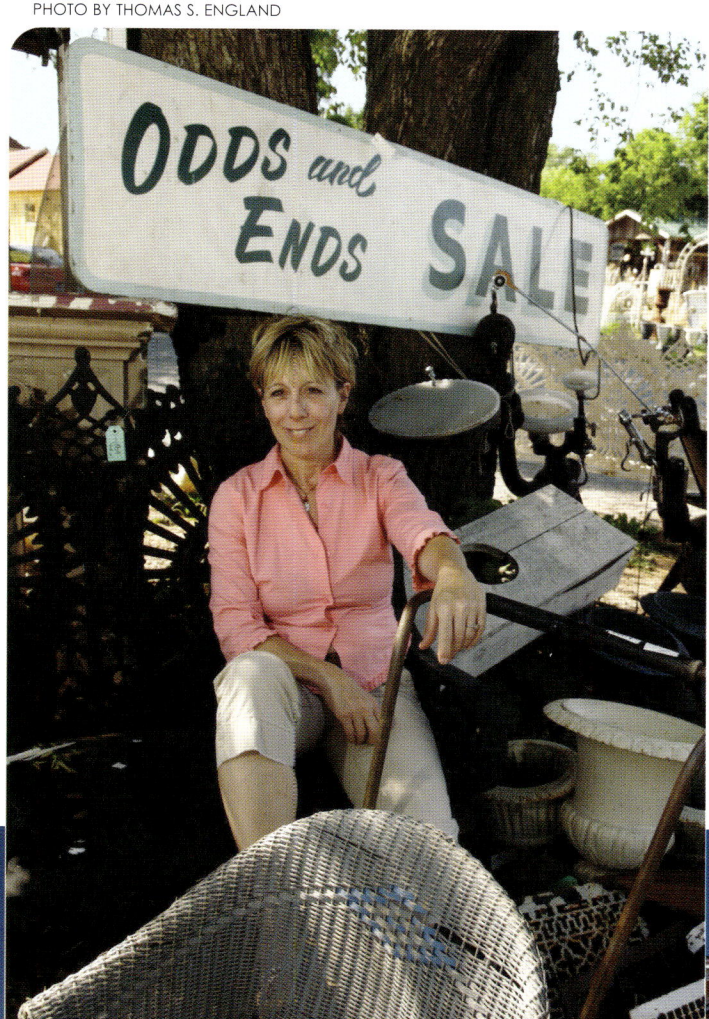

It's an adventure just looking around at the Old Lucketts Store, a collection of over twenty antique dealers selling everything from furniture and garden accents to ironworks and linen. Located in a restored three-story, 1910 structure that once served as a post office, general store, and home, the store is a dream come true for owner Suzanne Eblen (shown here), who started by selling dinettes out of a barn. With finds in every corner and flea-market pricing, Lucketts has drawn the attention of national publications and been voted the best antique shop in the county.

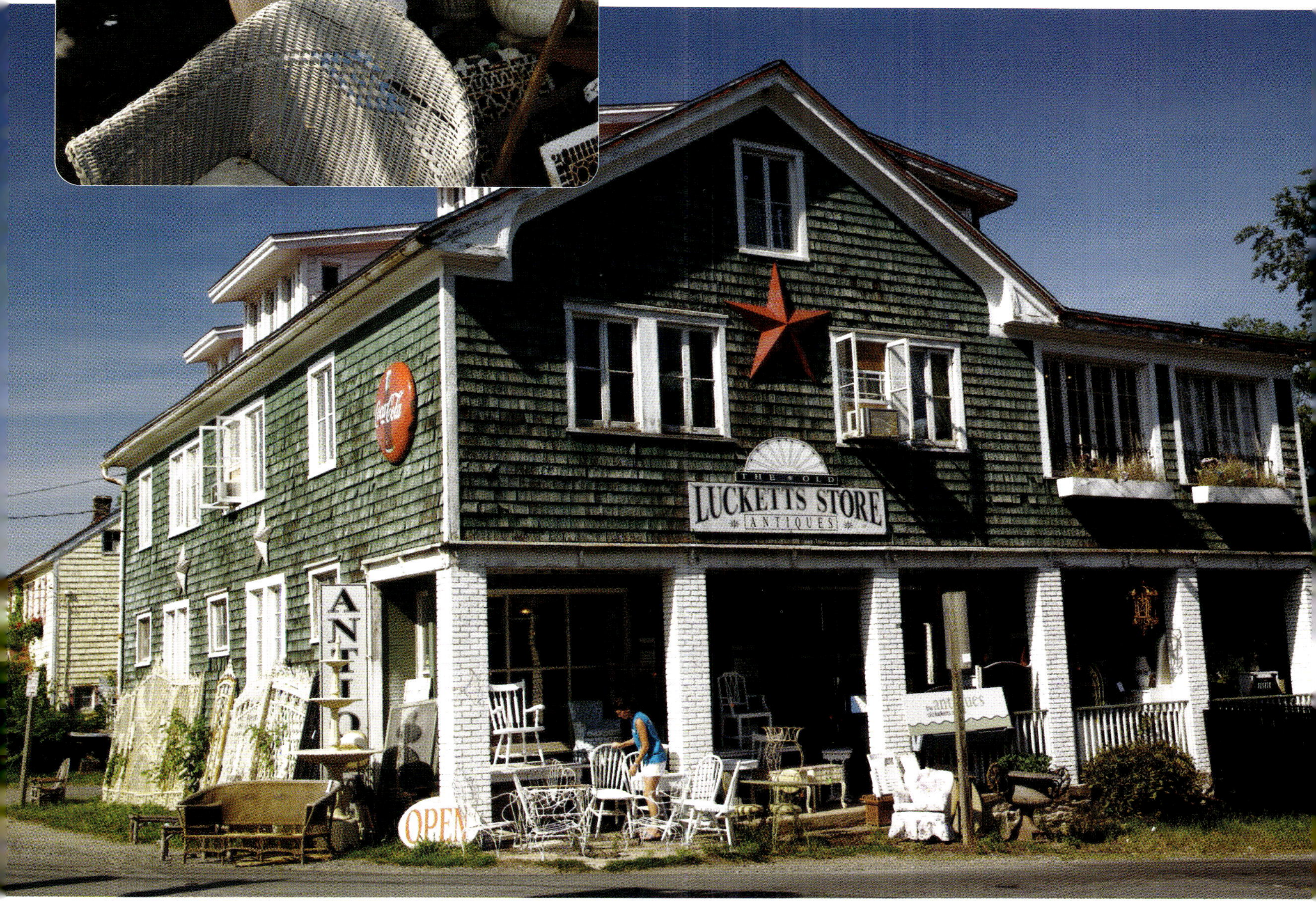

PHOTO BY THOMAS S. ENGLAND

PHOTO BY JEANETTE BURKLE

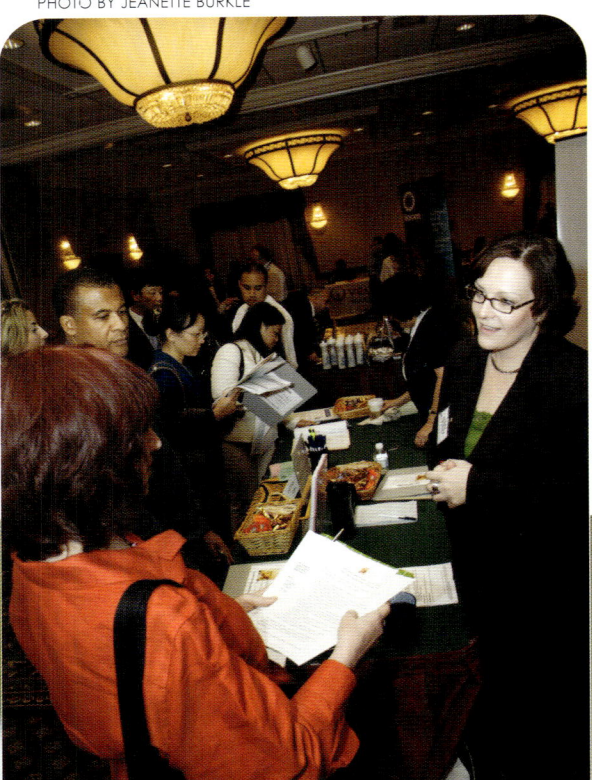

The Loudoun Chamber's semi-annual Job Fair has helped a diverse spectrum of employers find valued employees.

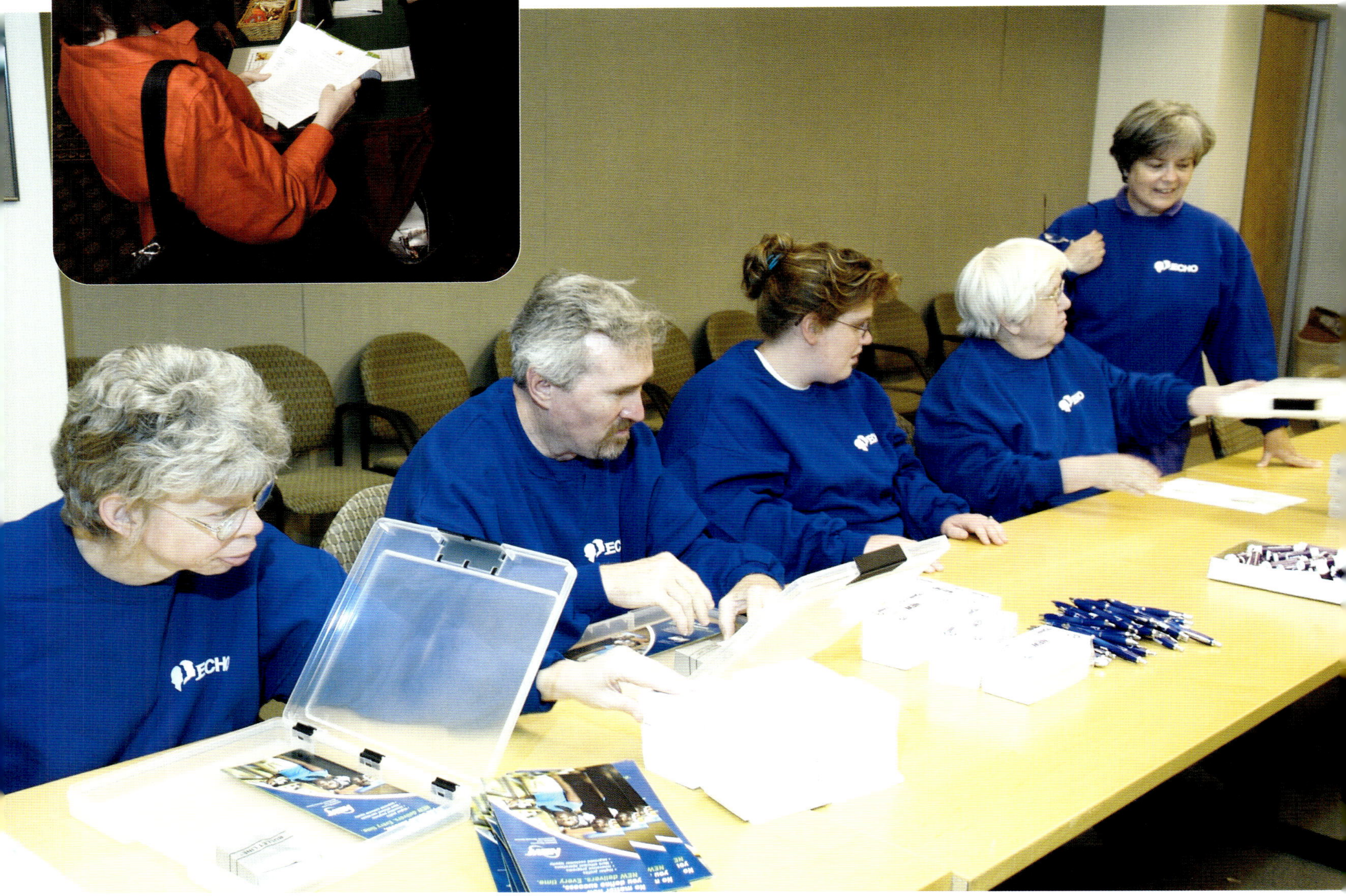

PHOTO BY THOMAS S. ENGLAND

ECHO, which stands for Every Citizen Has Opportunities, is a nonprofit organization that provides evaluation, training, and job options for challenged and disabled residents of Loudoun County. Working under the auspices of Mental Retardation Services, ECHO makes it possible for people in the program to find useful employment and helps employers who need extra help in peak production periods. After going through evaluation, vocational training, and work adjustment training, ECHO participants are placed in sheltered employment and mobile work crews. This group is working at Customer Service Companies, Inc. The company is the nation's leading provider of extended service contracts and buyer protection programs. The ECHO crew helps with sorting in the mail room.

No matter where you look in downtown Leesburg, there are both large and small reminders of history. The town has been serving as the center of government and commerce for Loudoun County since 1758 when it was first established. A stroll beginning at the Loudoun Museum, which is next door to Town Hall, gives visitors a chance to get an intimate picture of the history and the architecture of Leesburg. The Leesburg Heritage: Celebrating and Preserving Character makes sure the unique character of the community is maintained, from quaint window boxes to major landmarks. At one time during the War of 1812, Leesburg was the temporary capital of the United States. Throughout its history, the town has been linked to famous people, such as President James Monroe, who lived just south of town and who wrote the Monroe Doctrine in 1823. In the twentieth century, General George C. Marshall—the architect of the famous Marshall Plan, which rebuilt Europe after World War II—lived in Leesburg. Popular radio personality Arthur Godfrey, who dominated the airwaves in the 1940s and early '50s, lived in Leesburg and donated the land for the town's first airport.

It's a Matter of Trust

Providing protection behind the scenes

There is a company that has been in business since 1983, has its headquarters in Sterling, Virginia, and is so good at what it does, it has been recognized by J.D. Power and Associates for providing "An Outstanding Customer Service Experience," and yet it is virtually unknown to its end users.

The company is N.E.W. Customer Service Companies, Inc. (*NEW*), and it is the nation's leading provider of extended service contracts and buyer protection programs for consumer products.

"You may have never heard of *NEW*, but without a doubt you have shopped at a retailer that offers our service plans," said Fred Schaufeld, founder and chairman of *NEW*. "Our clients are major retailers and manufacturers, and they trust us to take care of their customers during a critical time—when a product isn't working and is in need of service.

"Taking care of the customer plays a significant role in *NEW*'s business," Schaufeld explained. "However, we don't stop with the customer. We work hard to be a great employer, to give back to the communities we work in, and to be a solid business partner to our clients. We realize that the better you take care of people, whether it is a customer, employee, client, or member of the community, the better the outcome for everyone."

NEW places a strong emphasis on caring for its employees and has created a working environment that is professional and fun, and which promotes a healthy personal and professional balance. This culture is evident in the many employee activities and community outreach programs at *NEW*.

PHOTO BY THOMAS S. ENGLAND

Since opening its doors in 1983, *NEW* has focused exclusively on producing results for clients through innovative programs, superior product protection, and unmatched customer care. Here at its headquarters in Dulles, the company continues to redefine the industry with innovations that raise the level of customer care and enhance brand loyalty.

PHOTO BY THOMAS S. ENGLAND

NEW Customer Service Companies, Inc. chairman Fred Schaufeld has a good reason to smile. A recent study conducted by an independent research organization reports that *NEW* leads the industry in delivering higher levels of customer satisfaction and loyalty for its clients. As the nation's leading provider of extended service contracts and buyer protection programs, *NEW* is headquartered in Dulles, Virginia. The company operates eight communications centers and has more than three thousand employees nationwide.

"We have over three thousand full-time employees, and we still celebrate birthdays each month," said Schaufeld. "We also believe in recognizing and rewarding employees for their performance. We have great recognition programs that reward individuals—both monthly and annually—for their motivation and contributions."

NEW also has many family-friendly events. They hold holiday parties and kick off the summer with a family picnic. Each Halloween, they decorate their offices and cubicles, transforming *NEW* into an "over-the-top" haunted mansion and invite children in to trick-or-treat.

At Christmas, Santa and Mrs. Claus visit and take pictures with the children (and some adults). Children also visit *NEW* for a "day of work" where they enjoy a morning of activities followed by lunch and a graduation ceremony, complete with a certificate of completion *and* a paycheck.

Children outside the company are also touched by *NEW*. Although it may be invisible to the general public, *NEW* is very much in evidence in the community. Students enrolled in three area schools' Head Start program know *NEW* employees personally because they read to the children weekly.

The company also provides Head Start with financial support that helps purchase multiple language books and fund field trips. "Since 1994 when *NEW* asked for our first wish list, they've been wonderful," said Holly Sontz, family community partnership support.

"We realize that the better you take care of people, whether it is a customer, employee, client, or member of the community, the better the outcome for everyone."

continued on page 118

More than likely, that friendly voice you hear when calling about a manufacturer's warranty or an extended service plan belongs to an employee at *NEW*. The company's contact centers handle more than 10 million consumer faxes, emails, and telephone calls in a typical year. *NEW*'s advanced call center application reduces the time a caller spends on the phone, a definite plus.

PHOTO BY THOMAS S. ENGLAND

continued from page 117

"Just recently they helped us get a specialized camera, which we use in mandatory eye testing, and a simultaneous translation machine so family members can follow what's going on at our meetings. But the best thing is that they have more volunteers just waiting for opportunities to help out."

Loudoun Cares is another community program that *NEW* supports. This past year, one of *NEW*'s initiatives was to help Loudoun Cares provide financial support to families struggling to pay winter heating bills. "*NEW* is helping raise awareness and showing the kind of philanthropic leadership that encourages others to step up and make a difference," said Andy Johnston, executive director of Loudoun Cares.

When a consumer purchases an extended service plan in a retail store, chances are that service plan is administered by *NEW*. Because of *NEW*'s outstanding service, they build exceptional customer loyalty for the retail outlet. For more than twenty years, *NEW* has provided postsale consumer care for many of the nation's largest retailers, manufacturers, and service firms.

PHOTO BY THOMAS S. ENGLAND

Being recognized once by J.D. Power and Associates for delivering "An Outstanding Customer Service Experience" is wonderful. Being recognized two years in a row is truly a cause for celebration. "We are very pleased with this recognition," said Fred Schaufeld, chairman and CEO of *NEW*. "This acknowledges our sustained commitment to delivering outstanding service on behalf of our clients and is a testament to the unwavering dedication to service excellence of our call center employees."

FHOTO BY THOMAS S. ENGLAND

NEW also has a working relationship with Every Citizen Has Opportunities (ECHO). This nonprofit organization provides a work environment to evaluate, train, and place mentally and physically challenged adults in supported employment. *NEW* contracts with them to help with packaging and mailing projects.

"We make a special effort to not only be good corporate citizens in dealing with our clients, but for the company and our employees to be good corporate citizens in the Loudoun area," Schaufeld adds. "We're involved with the Inova Fairfax and Loudoun Hospitals as well as Children's Hospital in Washington, D.C., the American Red Cross Blood Drive, Daffodil Day to support the American Cancer Society, making donations and building homes for Habitat for Humanity, as well as things like annual coat drives and school supply collections."

Considering that the company employs over three thousand people nationwide, protects the purchases of more than 100 million consumers annually, and works with a wide variety of community agencies and programs, perhaps *NEW* is not so invisible after all. ✦

It is time to rejoice when a home service technician shows up at your address, on time, and armed with the knowledge to fix the appliance or device that is no longer working properly. Customers with a manufacturer's warranty or a retailer's extended service plan administrated by *NEW* Customer Service Companies Inc. have come to expect that kind of service as the norm

PHOTO BY THOMAS S. ENGLAND

In Ashburn Village, the Loudoun County Sheriff's Office goes out of its way to make sure its deputies get to know the villagers and their needs. Sixteen law enforcement officers comprise the department's Bicycle Patrol Team. By being able to patrol areas not easily accessible by car, the deputies are better able to meet more people and build relationships, as well as keep a watchful eye out for the safety and well-being of everyone. Deputies, who volunteer for this duty in conjunction with their normal patrol responsibilities, also appreciate the fresh air and exercise the shift on the bike offers.

PHOTO BY JEANETTE BURKLE

We're Banking on You

From good relations come strong neighborhoods

Mercantile Potomac Bank is more than a local financial institution; it is a trusted neighbor and business confidant.

That's because this homegrown community bank has always understood that building relationships is the key to successful growth. Operating on the principles of Speed, Caring, Trust, and Responsiveness, Mercantile Potomac Bank helps individuals and businesses alike grow and prosper.

Founded in 1959, Mercantile Potomac Bank is a $3 billion community bank serving clients in northern Virginia, Montgomery County, Maryland, and Washington, D.C. In 2006, Mercantile Potomac Bank integrated James Monroe Bank into its family and now has five of its thirty-two total banking centers serving Loudoun County.

Mercantile Potomac is an affiliate of Mercantile Bankshares Corporation, a financial holding company with $17 billion in assets whose membership comprises thirteen community banks, a thriving investment and wealth management business, a mortgage company, and a full-service brokerage house. As an affiliate of Mercantile Bankshares Corporation and a division of Mercantile-Safe Deposit and Trust Company, Mercantile Potomac Bank is able to draw on regional resources for its clientele.

But while Mercantile Potomac Bank is backed by such distinctive financial strength, it remains guided by local decisions. The bank maintains a level of autonomy augmented by experienced, community-based management. Answers are given right at home, by people who know and understand each client's situation.

As a full-service community bank, Mercantile Potomac Bank offers a complete range of checking, savings, loan, and cash management options for individuals and businesses alike. In addition, through its Mercantile Investment & Wealth Management division, the bank provides a comprehensive array of products designed to ensure a secure future.

But with all its products and services, Mercantile Potomac Bank knows that one of the best ways to help clients is to retain its hallmark flexibility. "Speed, Caring, Trust, and Responsiveness" is more than a tagline; it's simply a way that associates at Mercantile Potomac Bank embrace each interaction with their clients. Rather than force clients to accept services that don't quite fit, Mercantile Potomac Bank is known for looking outside its product mix for tailored solutions that benefit all parties involved. Its goal, after all, is to help clients prosper, personally and professionally.

continued on page 124

Our goal is to help clients prosper, personally and professionally.

Left to right: Ken Cook, president of Mercantile Potomac Bank; O. Leland Mahan, Esq.; Richard Vaaler of Vaaler Real Estate; Robert Sevila, Esq., of Sevila, Saunders, Huddleston & White; and Paul Bice, senior vice president of Mercantile Potomac Bank, gather in downtown Leesburg for a client reception hosted by the bank.

At Mercantile Bank's quarterly Community Shred event, a partnership with NBC4-WRC and Shred-It, some eighty thousand pounds of paper are shredded on site before being recycled. In the past year, the bank has recycled enough paper to fill a football field sixteen feet tall.

Each year, Mercantile Bank helps sponsor the Bluemont Concert Series, presenting a wide variety of school concerts, workshops, and assemblies; performances in hospitals and nursing homes; public concerts on the green; old-time country dances; and special events around the region. A private nonprofit, Bluemont's wonderful and affordable events have become part of the fabric of life in communities throughout Virginia.

continued from page 123

For Mercantile Potomac, helping others is viewed as a sacred trust that goes beyond the working day. As community members themselves, the people of Mercantile Potomac understand that their participation in their neighborhoods directly impacts everyone's quality of life. By being a part of activities that benefit all segments of the community, these bankers get to know, firsthand, the needs and concerns of the neighbors they see every day.

In fact, listening to constituents' worries about identity theft led the bank to begin Community Shred days, a quarterly gathering that draws over a thousand people bearing tens of thousands of pounds of paper and personal effects to be shredded on site. Provided as a community service, the event is just one way the bank helps clients feel safe and secure. Whether it's thousands of hours of volunteer work or financial donations for causes of every sort, Mercantile Potomac believes that giving back is the best way to repay the trust clients show every day. ✦

As one of Loudoun County's most active community participants, Moore Cadillac Hummer lends its time, money, and facilities to a variety of local events and initiatives. Here, the dealership hosts a Chamber of Commerce mixer inside one of its spacious showrooms.

PHOTO BY DAVID GALEN

Humans are not the only ones who enjoy a day at the pool. The North Virginia Animal Swim Center caters to the needs of horses and dogs requiring aquatic rehabilitation and conditioning. Originally part of a Thorough-bred training facility, the present center was refurbished and opened to trainers and owners in 1989 by Roger Collins and Laura Hayward. The NVASC is located on forty-three acres approximately forty-five miles west of Washington amidst locales for foxhunting and internationally renowned horse shows. Swimming provides low-risk, low-impact exercise for horses that need conditioning or that are recovering from surgery. It builds muscles and expands and strengthens the heart and lungs. Horses have a natural ability to swim and usually become comfortable in the water in the first several swimming sessions. Dogs are one of the few animals that swim just for the pure pleasure of it. In the main pool, they can swim in fifty-yard laps or swim freely to retrieve, train, or just have fun. Fifty yards around, twelve feet deep, and containing 180,000 gallons of water, the NVASC is one of the largest facilities of its kind in America. Dogs swim in a slightly smaller pool, but either way it's great exercise—and nobody has to worry about sunscreen.

With the state's largest and the nation's third-largest horse population, there's no doubt that a big part of Loudoun County is horse country. As a $78 million-a-year business, the equine industry not only includes owners, horse farms, and horse races and trials, but also a network of related support industries. One of those is Moore Cadillac Hummer, whose Hummers provide horse owners not only with a stylish ride, but also a sturdy and reliable means of transportation for their four-footed friends.

PHOTO BY THOMAS S. ENGLAND

PHOTO BY BRUCE R. FEELEY

Connecting with the Global Economy

An investment in Dulles is an investment in Loudoun County

Together Ronald Reagan Washington National Airport and Washington Dulles International Airport service the capacity crowd of a Super Bowl stadium daily. Each year, the equivalent of the total population of the Metropolitan Washington region *times seven* utilizes the services of these 24/7 facilities. Collectively, they provide nearly thirty thousand jobs, generate business revenue of approximately $6.5 billion, and contribute more than $325 million in state and local taxes. One organization oversees them both: the Metropolitan Washington Airports Authority (MWAA).

The two entities are not only essential transportation hubs, but are vital to the local economy. Explains James E. Bennett, President and CEO of the MWAA, "We take the Metro Washington region—which includes northern Virginia and Loudoun County—and provide access to this global economy." The role of the MWAA, an independent body created by the Commonwealth of Virginia and the District of Columbia, is to design, plan, develop, and maintain access to the global aviation system for the Metropolitan Washington region. Put another way, the MWAA invests in the two airports to secure the economic well-being of northern Virginia and Loudoun County.

Washington Dulles International Airport has a unique history of vision and growth. When it opened in 1962, it was the first U.S. airport built for commercial jet aircraft at a time when airline travelers were in a distinct minority and air travel was still perceived as an exotic form of transportation to faraway places. But increases in passenger jet travel made

Washington Dulles International is the site of a $4 billion capital construction project to prepare the airport to serve the region's future needs.

aviation a prominent fixture of the economy of the nation and Loudoun County. The airport has truly shaped the community around it. The Dulles Corridor, which began as a highway to connect the Washington Beltway to the airport, has become a destination, as well as a catalyst for positive growth.

To secure Dulles's position for the future, the MWAA is overseeing a $4 billion capital construction project. "We're essentially in the process of rebuilding the airport. We're adding capacity and the facilities necessary for the airport to continue to serve the region," he says. Significant improvements include constructing an underground train system that will connect passengers from ticketing lobbies to the gates, building new parking facilities and new runways that will allow for expansion of the number of flights, expanding the entrance roadways to relieve congestion, expanding the terminal and enhancing passenger amenities like shops and restaurants, and continuing to improve security checkpoints. "The people of Loudoun County have supported this airport for more than forty years, and it has served the community well," says Bennett. "As we continue to grow, Loudoun County will continue to benefit from an economic and quality-of-life perspective, and Dulles will continue to proudly serve the region for the next forty years or more." ✦

"As we continue to grow, Loudoun County will continue to benefit from an economic and quality-of-life perspective."

Reagan Washington National airport efficiently serves the region with flights to seventy destinations.

PHOTO BY SCOTT INDERMAUR

IN MEMORY OF THE
CONFEDERATE SOLDIERS
OF LOUDOUN COUNTY VA.
ERECTED MAY 28, 1908

Loudoun County has had three courthouses, each with its own claim to fame. The first one was built in 1758. It was a brick building, forty feet by twenty-eight feet, that cost 365 pounds. The Declaration of Independence was read on the steps of the first courthouse during August Court Days of 1776. It was the first reading of the document anywhere in the state of Virginia. The second courthouse came along in 1811. It was also brick and was adorned with four large, beautiful stone pillars. Remnants of these can be seen in today's courtyard. Although there was a shootout between Yankee and Confederate soldiers on the front lawn, the courthouse survived nearly thirty years after the Civil War. The courthouse that stands today was erected in 1895. It has four columns and double doors, and is capped by a clock and a bell housed in the tower. The statue of a Confederate soldier that stands in front of the courthouse is a memorial to the many Rebel soldiers who died during the war. Stocks and whipping posts on the grounds remind visitors of the harsh measures of past law enforcement.

Navigating the Road to Success

Offering career management services for individuals and companies

Built on the belief that the road to professional success is best traveled with an experienced guide, Miles LeHane Companies—through its two operating divisions, Miles LeHane Group and Cornerstone HR Consulting—has become a world-class provider of career management services that include career transition, executive coaching, training and development, and human resources consulting.

Unique to Miles LeHane Companies is its headquarters in the graciously restored Glenfiddich House, an 1840s mansion that serves as a tranquil in-residence retreat for executives progressing into a new stage in their careers. Within this setting, Miles LeHane's experienced coaches, counselors, and consultants help direct individuals along a path of personal and professional reflection.

Miles LeHane's experienced coaches, counselors, and consultants help direct individuals along a path of personal and professional reflection.

PHOTO BY ALAN S. WEINER

Owners David and Melanie Miles, with Max, in front of Glenfiddich House, the antebellum mansion that serves as an in-residence retreat for executives transitioning to a new stage in their career.

Minimizing the stress of downsizing or organizational restructuring is a key Miles LeHane specialty. Through its outplacement and career transition services, the company has developed an enviable reputation for structuring and implementing career transition programs for all levels of staff from the day of separation activities through the consultative process, and not concluding until affected individuals have begun new employment.

In fact, with the speed of business stretching the limits of professional skills, Miles LeHane's owners, David and Melanie Miles, provide coaching for employees at all levels through its Cornerstone HR Consulting operating division. Cornerstone works alongside the client stakeholders to develop clear goals, then develops an action plan that serves as a roadmap for transforming people and organizations.

For clients faced with outsourcing their human resource needs, the Cornerstone HR Consulting division offers Web-based assessment tools, used alone or with a personal coach, that focus on everything from personality profiles to compliance training to leadership development. The available online tools also give program participants and their corporate stakeholders easy access to a range of training and career search systems.

When the road to success gets a little rough, it is good to have Miles LeHane Companies along to help navigate around the obstacles and avoid the detours. ✦

American Home Mortgage loan consultant Tammy Wilt at the Annual Reston Taste of the Town Festival signs up a potential home buyer for a service offered through AHM's contract with a real estate company. The service is free Web-based software that enables buyers to search for homes nationwide.

VIRGINIA WINES
A Growing Tradition

Charming and picturesque, Leesburg offers its nearly thirty thousand residents the best of both worlds. Located about forty miles northwest of Washington, D.C., the small town, which also serves as the county seat, has the advantage of offering residents quick and easy access to the nation's capital, while also serving as a residential sanctuary from all the hustle and bustle.

Building Lifetime Communities

A place for generations to put down roots

As Americans continue to seek the American Dream—home ownership—a sense of community becomes increasingly important. A sense of community provides what was once a small-town feel. As quality of life grows in importance, having a homestead and a community becomes very important. What may seem like Utopia is becoming a reality, thanks to Greenvest L.C., the builder of lifetime communities.

"We are a residential builder of well-planned communities," explains Packie E. Crown, vice president of planning and zoning with Greenvest. "We saw a niche that wasn't being addressed in planned communities. In order to either expand living space or downsize, families typically had to move out of the area. The concept for The Villages at Dulles South is to create four distinct communities which provide a place for generations of Loudoun's families to put down roots."

Over the next twenty years, Greenvest is planning to build approximately fifteen thousand housing units. The four communities, or villages, will occupy 4,200 acres and are wrapped in hiking trails, recreation areas, and green spaces, including a golf course. This plan will help to provide housing for some of the 110,000-plus households projected to move to Loudoun County by 2030, according to the Council on Governments (COG).

Each of the four villages—Arcola, Lenah, Broad Run, and Greenfields—will have a distinct character.

Arcola includes a 123-acre George Mason University campus, the George Mason Town Center, and an elementary school.

The Village of Lenah will include an educational nature center along with a middle school. Approximately 30 percent of the housing units located here will be workforce housing dedicated to those who are so essential to our communities—teachers, firefighters, and law enforcement, health-care, and other workers.

The Village at Broad Run features an age-restricted community. A golf course and open space serve as buffers along its western edge. A retail center, community/recreation center, and elementary school complete this village.

Three schools, upscale shopping, recreation facilities, and office space give the Village at Greenfields all of the benefits and conveniences of a self-contained community.

Communities such as these will drive Loudoun's economic engine into 2030 and reduce traffic by providing residents with everything they need within their community. Greenvest also proposes the use of Community Development Authority bonds (CDAs) as a financing tool that has been used successfully across the country. CDAs will finance up-front the construction of roads, schools, a 200-acre park, and infrastructure without impacting the county's debt capacity.

Greenvest is building lifetime communities by using a cutting-edge approach and forward thinking. The company has looked at the best models across the country and brought the best ideas to its Loudoun communities. Greenvest has made a major commitment to Loudoun County's future. ✦

Greenvest is building lifetime communities by using a cutting-edge approach and forward thinking.

Greenvest L.C. is a name that stands for the highest standards and the creation of better living environments and lifestyles founded in traditional American small towns. Town centers and village greens, recreation areas and walking trails, all contribute to the unhurried appeal of Greenvest's lifetime communities.

Farsighted homebuilders, home buyers, architects, land planners, designers, engineers, and financial institutions are unified in their association with Greenvest to deliver the best in master plans for townhomes and single-family dwellings. Greenvest L.C. is renowned for its team approach, which brings unique, professional depth and scope to all its endeavors.

BUTCHERS & GRAZIER

ORGANIC MEATS & POU

PHOTO BY BRUCE R. FEELEY

DRY
GOODS

At any given time of day, mouth-watering aromas fill Middleburg's Home Farm Store. Freshly brewed coffee, just-baked pastries, and oven-roasted organic vegetables are just some of the tempting items offered at this traditional butcher shop and grazier. Located in the old bank building at the traffic light in the center of Middleburg, Home Farm Store features locally raised beef, veal, lamb, poultry, and pork, much of it USDA Certified Organic; all of it is Certified Humanely Raised. The shop also carries a full complement of groceries, sweets, cookbooks, and cast-iron cookware, and ice cream treats are regularly served up at the old-fashioned soda fountain.

ROASTED AYRSHIRE BEETS $5⁹⁵/lb

Three centuries tell the story of the historic Ayrshire Farm. The original plantation house on the one-thousand-acre property was built circa 1821. Today, the certified organic farm is producing livestock and crops in a sustainable, yet profitable manner. Ayrshire specializes in rare and endangered breeds of livestock, like the White Park cattle, purely descended from the herd sequestered at Chillingham, Northumberland, England, in the thirteenth century. John Hass wanders among the creatures with the wise and knowing, but gentle-looking faces. The farm also raises Shire horses, another ancient and rare breed. The Shires provide horse-powered skill in the constant task of soil improvement for the many heirloom fruits and vegetables grown on the farm. Aryshire is also focused on the future of organic farming. 4-H students regularly work with the Shires' cattle and vegetable gardens as a part of an innovative program that allows suburban children to work with and exhibit farm animals and experience farm life. In addition, the farm partners with the International Exchange for Agriculture, an international organization that places apprentices from around the world in working farms. These programs may ensure that Aryshire will still be telling its story in the next century.

PHOTO BY THOMAS S. ENGLAND

Perfecting the Art of Communication

Connecting people to each other, to the Web, and to the world

For the thousands of people who pass by it every day, the sprawling AOL campus on the corner of Waxpool Road and Route 28 is easy to miss. The complex of buildings sports no blaring AOL signs or any other visible evidence that one of the world's largest Internet companies is in their midst.

But while AOL's buildings may be modest, the company's impact on the community since moving to Loudoun County ten years ago has been anything but.

More than four thousand people call the Dulles campus their workplace home. The ten buildings on this campus house the corporate headquarters, along with programming, marketing, business support, data center operations, technology and systems development, customer care support services, and a child-care center.

AOL's first twenty years were focused on becoming the world's largest subscription-based ISP service, emphasizing ease of use for the average consumer. The company was a pioneer of online safety, leading the way first with the introduction of online parental controls and later championing the fight against spam and hackers—becoming the first ISP in the industry to provide its members with free antivirus protection.

With the launch of AOL.com in the summer of 2005, AOL opened its content free to the Web, charting a new course for the company as one of the world's largest Web services companies. In the summer of 2006, AOL took the next step in this direction, making its email, software, unique programming content, safety and security tools, and other services free to anyone with a high-speed Internet connection.

AOL is also focused today on growing both its international presence and its brand, having recently launched portal services in Europe (United Kingdom, France, and Germany) and most recently introducing a Chinese language service as well as a portal in India. As of the fall of 2006, the company's network of Web brands—which include AOL.com, AIM, MapQuest, Moviefone, Netscape, ICQ, the AOL Latino service, Black Voices, KOL, and RED—attracts more than 110 million monthly visitors.

The company is also extending its leadership position in quality online video with the AOL Video portal, which includes everything from classic TV shows available free and on-demand to download-to-own movies and user-generated videos.

Just as AOL works to make the Internet a better experience, it is working to make its local community a better place for everyone who lives here. For example, AOL is a founding partner with

continued on page 144

The company was a pioneer of online safety, becoming the first ISP in the industry to provide its members with free antivirus protection.

AOL's sprawling Dulles campus features numerous employee amenities, including two state-of-the-art exercise facilities, three on-site cafeterias, all-day bistro service, a day-care center that houses 150 children while parents keep watch via webcam, bus service between buildings, and daily air shuttle service to and from NYC out of Dulles Airport.

PHOTO BY ALAN S. WEINER

PHOTOS BY ALAN S. WEINER

PHOTO BY ALAN S. WEINER

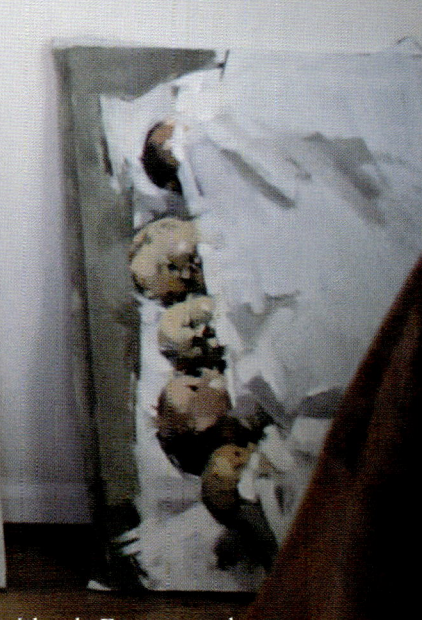

Maggie Siner's work has been described as "contemporary figurative painting which blends Eastern and Western influences, and displays lively calligraphic brush work and crystalline light." This blending of cultures comes from her years as a visiting professor of painting at Xiamen University in China, her time on the faculty of L'Institute d'Universites Americaines and the Lacoste School of Art in France, and her experience as artist-in-residence at the Savannah College of Art and Design and dean of the Washington Studio School in Washington, D.C. Her paintings, still lifes, and portraits often capture moments in daily life. She has lived and painted in Loudoun County for more than twenty-five years. During her annual summer trips to France, she teaches and paints just for herself. She is a respected painter of international renown, and her work has been exhibited in galleries throughout the United States and Europe. Siner's creations are also in private collections in this country, Canada, Britain, France, Italy, Switzerland, Germany, Sweden, the Netherlands, South Africa, Kenya, the Philippines, Indonesia, Japan, and, of course, China.

Keeping You Connected

Offering state-of-the-art telecommunications solutions

Today's advanced telephone systems provide more than just a way for people to communicate. A vast array of features like voice mail, call cost accounting, and automatic call distribution help businesses cut costs, boost productivity, and streamline their organization. But how does one go about choosing the right system?

Since 1983, Bridgman Communications, Inc. has been the local expert in supplying clients with affordable and effective solutions for their telecommunications needs. Located in Dulles, Bridgman is a professional interconnect telephone company with extensive experience in the sales, installation, maintenance, and relocation of telephone systems, voice mail, and related peripherals.

Bridgman believes that the purchase of a communications system or the maintenance of an existing system requires a long-term commitment from the supplier. It's a commitment that defines the company's unparalleled quality of customer service.

"We provide the highest-quality, most consistent service possible," says president and CEO Georgia Graves. "Our knowledgeable staff has a proven track record in the industry and are able to provide clients with professional, efficient, and prompt handling of their requests—twenty-four hours a day, seven days a week."

Because there is no such thing as one-size-fits-all in telecommunications, Bridgman's involvement doesn't begin with a sale, but with a consultation. And it ends with a complete turnkey arrangement that includes engineering support, programming, cabling, installation, and complete customer training. The purchase agreement also includes a host of after-sale support services, including full maintenance for one year and guaranteed four-hour emergency response time.

PHOTO BY SCOTT INDERMAUR

PHOTO BY SCOTT INDERMAUR

Bridgman's Technology Team reviews the Data Center set-up for Voice and Data Applications at ARGroup's Corporate Offices in Leesburg. This team effort consistently results in successful system installation, implementation, and evaluation through project completion. Left to right: senior technical engineer Bob Cunningham, operations manager Jim Strube, software programming engineer Dayan Nawaratne, installation technical supervisor Gerald Bridgman, and customer service manager Seema Varma.

"Customers trust our organization because we take total responsibility as the single point of contact," continues Graves, "even if the problem isn't within the product we sold." For instance, Bridgman handles issues with customers' chosen dial-tone-services carriers (for example, Verizon) and works in partnership with other technology vendors.

Not only has Bridgman supported systems from over seventeen telephone manufacturers, its products are designed with the built-in ability to handle current and future needs on a platform that delivers today's technology with minimum cost to seamlessly upgrade to new features as they become available.

Furthermore, Bridgman specializes in integrating companies with multiple locations through IP technology. They provide integration that makes all locations work as though they are under one roof, even if a few blocks or thousands of miles may separate them. This can make a company's operations seamless between locations, offer tremendous savings, and enhance the ability to interface easily with employees and customers without geographic limitations. While many manufacturers offer IP products, those made by Inter-Tel Incorporated, a well-respected manufacturer of telephone equipment, provide the most comprehensive, user-friendly, and seamless applications in the marketplace today.

Due to these and other revolutionary developments in the telecommunications industry, Bridgman naturally anticipates an increase in its growth in the upcoming years. Most importantly, the company looks forward to helping other Loudoun County businesses and organizations operate more effectively with the best, most state-of-the-art telecommunication systems available today. ◆

Bridgman Communications installed an extensive phone system at Mount Vernon Estates and Gardens, the home of our first president, George Washington. The five-hundred-acre property includes thirty-three buildings, five homes, and a complete fire department. Left to right: president of Bridgman Communications Georgia Graves, administrative services manager Cynthia Fiscko, director of special projects James Simms, and executive director James Rees.

"Customers trust our organization because we take total responsibility as the single point of contact."

Ringman Delvin Helderman, from Sulphur, Oklahoma, assists the auctioneer in taking bids at the Angus Across America sale at the Whitestone Farms show barn. Whitestone is a registered Angus and Red Angus breeding farm about forty miles west of Washington, D.C. The seven-hundred-acre farm is owned by George Lemm, Marvin and Katheryn Robertson, and Tom and Nancy Andracsek. Another fifteen hundred acres of farm land are leased to accommodate the herd of pure-bred Angus stock. Each animal has a certificate from the American Angus Association verifying its pedigree. For twenty-five years Whitestone has been in business, and they currently host three auctions a year. The Angus Across America sale differs from others in that people who have purchased stock from Whitestone are invited back to sell the offspring of those animals. Whitestone is well known in the cattle industry and attracts buyers from throughout the United States and Canada, and from as far away as Australia and Argentina.

PHOTO BY DAVE GALEN

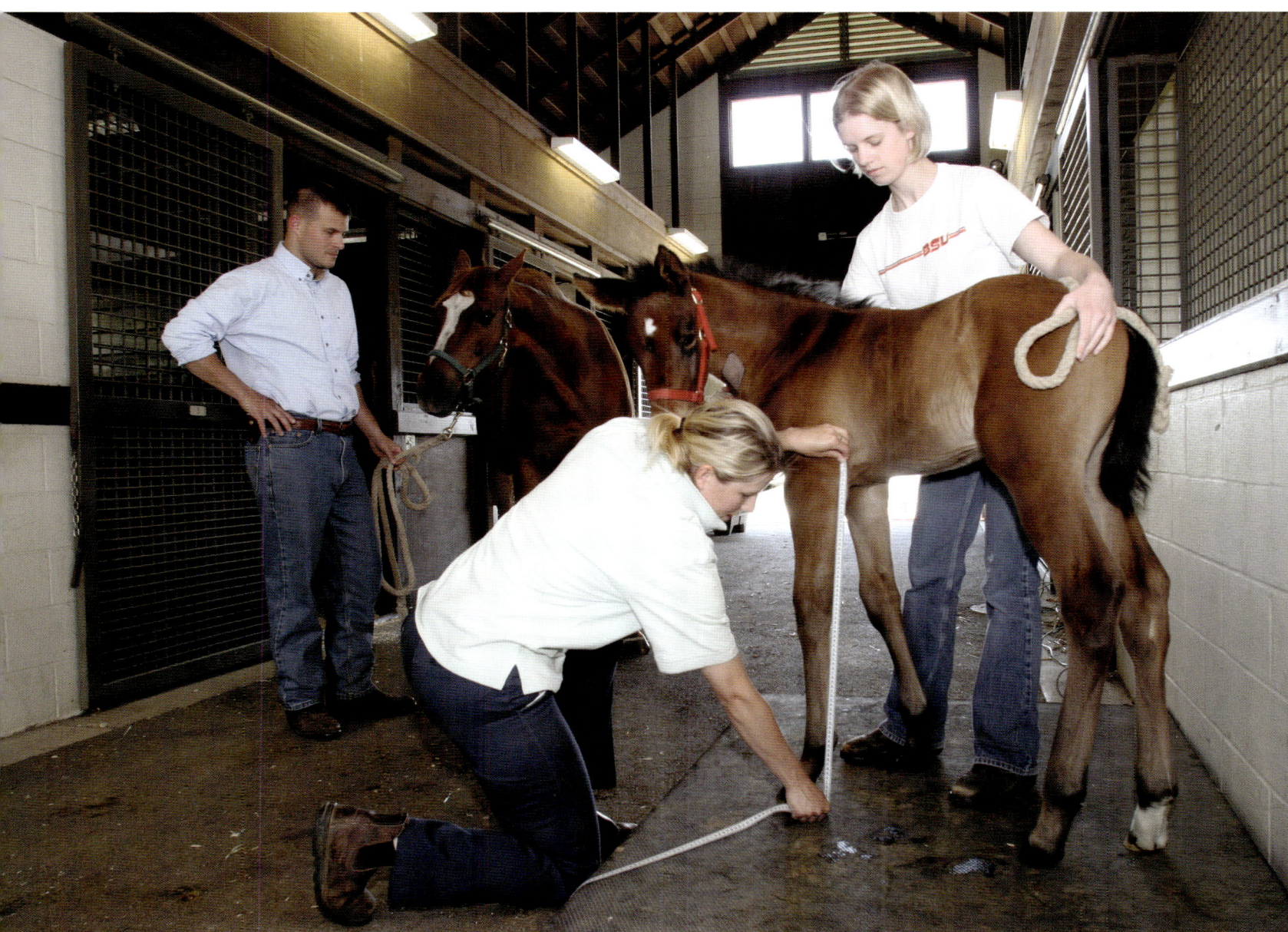

PHOTO BY ALAN S. WEINER

W. Burton Staniar, Tania Cubitt, and Lindsey George measure a colt at the Virginia Tech Middleburg Agricultural Research and Extension Center, a 420-acre farm dedicated to equine research. The center's work includes a study of a pasture supplement containing fiber and fat to determine the effects of these two ingredients on bone development and overall growth. Results of the study led to further research on metabolic regulation in the glucose-insulin system, using the horse as a model.

PHOTO BY BRUCE R. FEELEY

Building Engineering Intelligence

Making sense out of a complex world

M. C. Dean, Inc. is one the nation's leading systems engineering and integration firms specializing in complex power, electronics, and telecommunications systems for major government and commercial users. The firm has offices throughout the eastern United States and overseas, in Europe and Southwest Asia. Founded in 1949, M. C. Dean, Inc. has been headquartered in Loudoun County, Virginia, since 1982.

Complex systems require expertise, and the application of technical expertise to deliver unparalleled solutions for the nation's most challenging projects has driven the growth of M. C. Dean, Inc. and the development of its staff. Every day, the firm's nearly two thousand engineers, technicians, and administrative staff support the facilities, infrastructure, and organizations that are critical to our nation's future. M. C. Dean, Inc. professionals provide full-lifecycle engineering services for pharmaceutical and semiconductor manufacturing plants, large technology data centers, military facilities domestically and in theaters of combat, public transit infrastructures such as subway systems and airports, health-care campuses, resorts and hospitality facilities, and Fortune 1000 corporations.

An engineer for M. C. Dean, Inc.'s OpenBand subsidiary analyzes circuits in the Network Operations Center in Loudoun County. Thousands of OpenBand subscribers in Loudoun enjoy 100Mbps Internet, cable TV, and telephone on the fastest fiber optic network in the county.

Ensuring that its staff maintain mastery of the state-of-the-art is a priority for M. C. Dean, Inc., and, as such, the firm dedicates substantial resources to the effort. Chief among these is the company's dedicated Education Department, which operates M. C. Dean, Inc. University and coordinates adult education programs taught by M. C. Dean, Inc. professors and held at the firm's facilities. This formal instruction, combined with established career paths and opportunities to earn system-specific technical certifications in areas such as life safety and optical networking, allows the firm's employees to make the most of their capabilities.

Today's major clients require speed to market—and speed to market requires capacity, closely coordinated operations, and a focus on customer needs. M. C. Dean, Inc. is ranked among the Top 40 Specialty Contractors in the United States by *Engineering News Record*, and operates throughout the world. The firm's diversified operations work together in support of the most demanding clients, ensuring seamless integration and a single point of responsibility for related systems such as instrumentation and controls, grounding and critical power, command and control, homeland security and surveillance systems, and sensor systems. The firm provides analytical, networking, and applications development expertise in support of these disciplines.

continued on page 154

M. C. Dean, Inc. is actively involved in the economic vitality of the communities that the firm and its employees call home.

Electrical apprentices learn how to wire circuits at M. C. Dean, Inc.'s Dulles headquarters. The firm operates the region's largest electrical apprenticeship program, graduating fifty journeyman electricians each year.

PHOTO BY BRUCE R. FEELEY

Technicians field service requests from some of the one-thousand-plus D.C.-area clients for whom M. C. Dean, Inc. maintains electronic systems. The call center shown here is staffed around the clock and has operated continuously since its creation a decade ago.

PHOTO BY BRUCE R. FEELEY

continued from page 153

M. C. Dean, Inc. entered the competitive communications market in 1999 when the firm established the converged services provider OpenBand. OpenBand operates high-capacity optical networking, traditional switched networks, and global IP satellite services and frequently works with M. C. Dean, Inc. divisions to support application development and complex networking requirements.

M. C. Dean, Inc. is actively involved in the economic vitality of the communities that the firm and its employees call home. This is best exemplified by the company's workforce development efforts, which target those most in need of developing technical skills in the greater Washington, D.C., region. The firm is the largest corporate sponsor of state and city technical apprenticeship programs in the District of Columbia and the Commonwealth of Virginia, and routinely focuses its recruiting efforts in areas of high unemployment—seeking out those who show an aptitude for technical and craft work, and demonstrate a solid work ethic.

Additionally, M. C. Dean, Inc. participates in numerous community events and contributes to charitable organizations such as the Loudoun County Chapter of the Salvation Army, the Pentagon Memorial Fund, the Loudoun County Community Holiday Coalition, Grace Community Church, the Capital Area Minority Contractors Association, and many others. ✦

M. C. Dean, Inc. technical staff build the electrical systems for the Dulles Automated People Mover tunnels. Since the 1980s, the firm has been involved in numerous upgrades and expansions at Washington Dulles International Airport.

PHOTO BY BRUCE R. FEELEY

When the Town of Leesburg decided to redesign their city's Government Center in the mid-1980s, they made the project into a national design competition. Architects throughout the country were tasked with providing a solution to the oddly shaped site on Market Street, which is also surrounded by many historic buildings. Hanno Weber & Associates of Chicago won the competition with their beautiful, innovative, and functional complex, which includes a three-story block of town offices, an urban plaza, a parking garage, and the center's distinctive octagonal-shaped Town Hall. The project's unifying focal point, the Town Hall reflects the center's overall esthetic of classical architectural elements reinterpreted with a modern twist.

LEESBURG

PHOTO BY THOMAS S. ENGLAND

Rural industries flourish in Hillsboro and other regions of Loudoun County. One of the most noted in the area is winemaking. Wind down the country roads, and you're sure to find one of the area's wineries and a treat for your senses. Nestled amidst the rolling hills, the surroundings are serene and also provide the right climate, air, and water drainage for the vineyards. Drive with the windows down during the height of growing season, and you may even smell the unmistakable scent of grapes in the air. Be sure to stop in one of the wineries for a tour and taste. The county's wineries are the leading Virginia producers of vinifera and New World grape wines. Another well-known area wine is the Norton; using a dark-colored grape native to Virginia, the wine's fruity flavors may also include plums and tart cherries.

PHOTO BY SCOTT INDERMAUR

Where Clients Come First

Whatever your real estate needs, Access Realty is there

There's a reason business partners Kathy Samson and Steve Harrison named their real estate company Access Realty. For these two real estate professionals, the relationship between agent and client is all about accessibility. Whether it's taking calls seven days a week or establishing a conveniently located storefront in Old Town Leesburg across from the county seat's courthouse, Samson and Harrison, as well as the nearly thirty agents who work with them, have found numerous ways to make themselves available to clients practically around the clock.

"Our focus is on our clients. They always come first," says Harrison, who joined forces with Samson in 2001 to found Access Realty. Their goal was to create an organization that could serve clients comprehensively, meeting all of their real estate needs. They succeeded. Today, Access Realty specializes not only in residential home buying and home selling throughout Loudoun County and Virginia, but also in commercial real estate, land sales, and historic real estate, among other types of transactions. Furthermore, the company has taken its service to an entirely different level by having additional licenses to practice real estate in Maryland and Florida, giving clients access to a much larger geographic area when it comes to where they want to live.

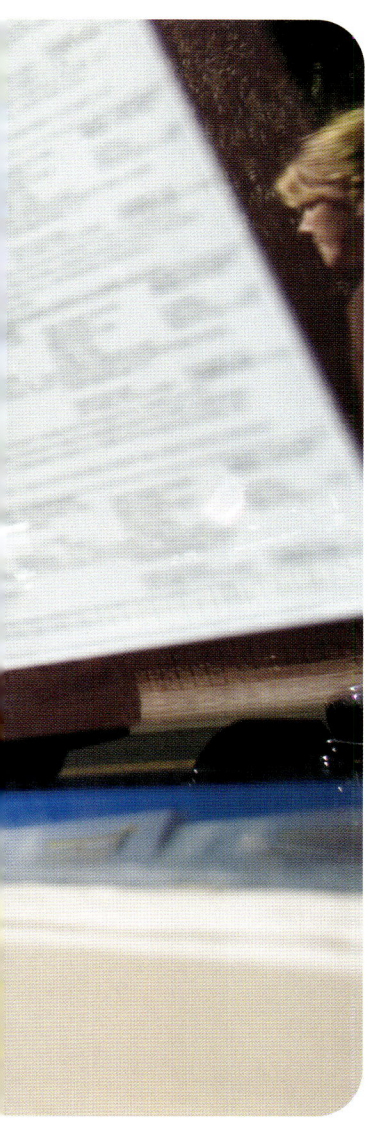

"When people are moving to this area, they often don't know which side of the river they want to live on. So we're able to help them whether they want to settle in Virginia or Maryland," notes Samson, who also serves as the company's broker. "We've also found that many people are purchasing second homes or retiring in Florida, so we decided to hold licenses there as well."

While it may sound challenging to work in three different real estate markets, Access Realty keeps a finger on the pulse of each one by studying it closely every day and complementing that knowledge with an impressive depth of experience in and keen understanding of the overall real estate industry—something that has become a hallmark for this ever-growing firm.

According to Samson, "We want to make the whole real estate process as smooth and painless as possible." So, everyone within the company, including owners Harrison and Samson, has also become well versed in areas like finance and building contracting. Additionally, they have cultivated valuable associations within each community and dedicated themselves not only to helping clients move through their real estate transactions seamlessly, but also to being their real estate company of choice long after the paperwork has been signed and filed away. In fact, many clients have enjoyed—and continue to enjoy— working with Access Realty on multiple transactions.

It's the same level of commitment Access Realty shows for Loudoun County, the community it calls home. From sponsoring Little League teams to participating in Leesburg's annual fall festival, the company is always there for its neighbors. Just like it is for its many happy clients. ✦

"Our focus is on our clients. They always come first."

For Steve Harrison and Kathy Samson, clients always come first. Staying true to that philosophy is the foundation upon which these two real estate professionals have been building their business since 2001. And today, Access Realty is one of Loudoun County's most successful and prolific real estate firms, helping buyers and sellers achieve their goals in both the residential and commercial arenas.

Families that turn to Access Realty not only are given the chance to realize their dreams of homeownership, but also are provided with all of the tools they need to make the residential home-buying process a seamless one. Each of Access Realty's agents is well versed in a variety of areas, from finance to building contracting. This range of knowledge lets clients know they are working with people who have their best interests in mind, from the moment they walk through door to the moment the papers are signed and filed away.

PHOTO BY SCOTT INDERMAUR

Entered into service sometime around 1800, White's Ferry remains the only working ferry still crossing the Potomac River. Originally named Conrad's Ferry after its founder, the ferry began as a passenger and cargo transport costing a rider, cattle, or carriage just pennies per trip. The ferry was purchased after the Civil War by lawman and business owner Elijah Viers White, who switched from rope to cable on the line that guides the barge in its crossing. A cable, accompanied by tug boats, still guides the barge today, which is used by commuters daily as a shortcut between Maryland and Virginia.

PHOTO BY ALAN S. WEINER

It's one of the busiest regions in the nation, and in many places, a river runs through it. Which means many bridges—from historic to modern—have been built to carry automobile and train traffic to and from points in Virginia and Maryland across the Potomac and into the Capital Region.

"I used to think these guys were just plain strange," says Tony Mallory, referring to the Civil War reenactment of the 1863 cavalry and artillery duel at Goose Creek. "But once I got recruited to join, it became a lot of fun. Not only do I get to be around other horsemen, I've made what I consider to be some of my very best friends." Mallory is one of several ex-military men and lifelong horse riders involved in re-creating this and other Civil War events about once a month. The Goose Creek battle reenactment is part of the Memorial Day weekend Hunt Country Stable Tour, a self-directed auto tour of the horse farms located in and around Upperville and Middleburg. Held each year since 1959, the tour benefits the outreach programs of Upperville's Trinity Episcopal Church.

Chapter Three

ENJOY!

Loudoun County may be business-oriented, but it also offers plenty of ways in which to play hooky from the fast lane. With a moderate year-round climate, beautiful outdoor scenery, and picturesque towns and villages, Loudoun regularly lures even the busiest of bees out from behind their desks and into the great outdoors.

Weekends are a great time to soak in some local color by exploring the area's many historic villages and towns. Places like Leesburg, Aldie, and Waterford each have their own unique character, which colors everything from their shops to their restaurants, as well as numerous harvest festivals, home and garden tours, and arts and crafts shows.

Over forty parks totaling hundreds of miles of recreational trails are big draws for walkers, runners, bikers, and in-line skaters. Those who prefer to recreate atop four feet will delight in the fact that much of Loudoun County is horse country. Not only are there plentiful places to ride, but numerous hunt clubs also provide equestrian enthusiasts with weekly opportunities to practice the fine art of hunting, jumping, and racing.

No discussion of recreation in Loudoun County would be complete without mentioning golf. The region is noted for over a dozen beautiful and challenging golf courses, many of which are designed by legends such as Arnold Palmer and Robert Trent Jones, and which have won accolades from top golf publications. Most recently, *Golf Magazine* named Lansdowne Resort's 36-hole, championship Greg Norman layout among the country's "Top 10 New Courses You Can Play." And Lansdowne itself is rapidly gaining in reputation as one of the region's best resort experiences.

Cultural attractions that combine history and art can be found throughout the county. Leesburg alone is home to such varied attractions as the Balls Bluff Battlefield Regional Park, Oatlands Plantation, Historic Morven Park, the Thomas Balch Library, and the Loudoun Museum. And some of the world's best shopping, dining, and cultural attractions are located in nearby Washington, D.C., only a forty-five-minute drive away.

Those initially attracted to Loudoun County for its economic opportunities will soon experience another of its charms: the ability to temper hard work with relaxation, play, and cultural enrichment.

PHOTO BY JEANETTE BURKLE

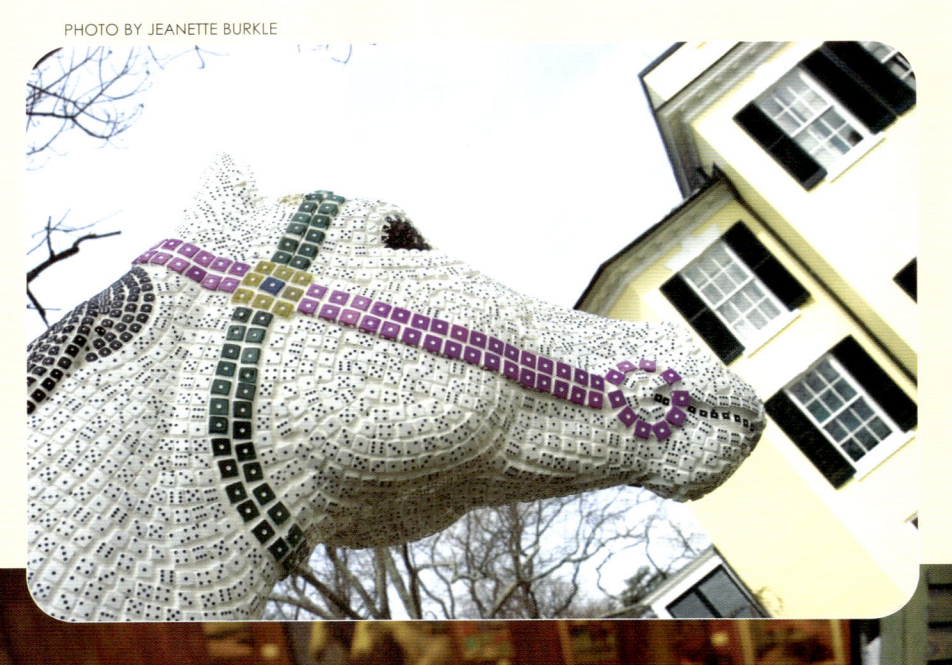

Fanciful horses from the Chamber's Horsing Around Loudoun public arts program were auctioned at historic Oatlands Plantation in March 2006. At the Oatlands Historic Mansion and Gardens, tea for two (or three, four, or more) is a terrific way to slow down the everyday pace and taste the flavors of good conversation with friends. The traditional afternoon tea held in the stately mansion's Carriage House begins at 1:00 p.m. sharp and features delicious sandwiches, sweets, and the Oatlands signature blend of tea. Guests often top off tea with a tour of the beautiful terraced gardens.

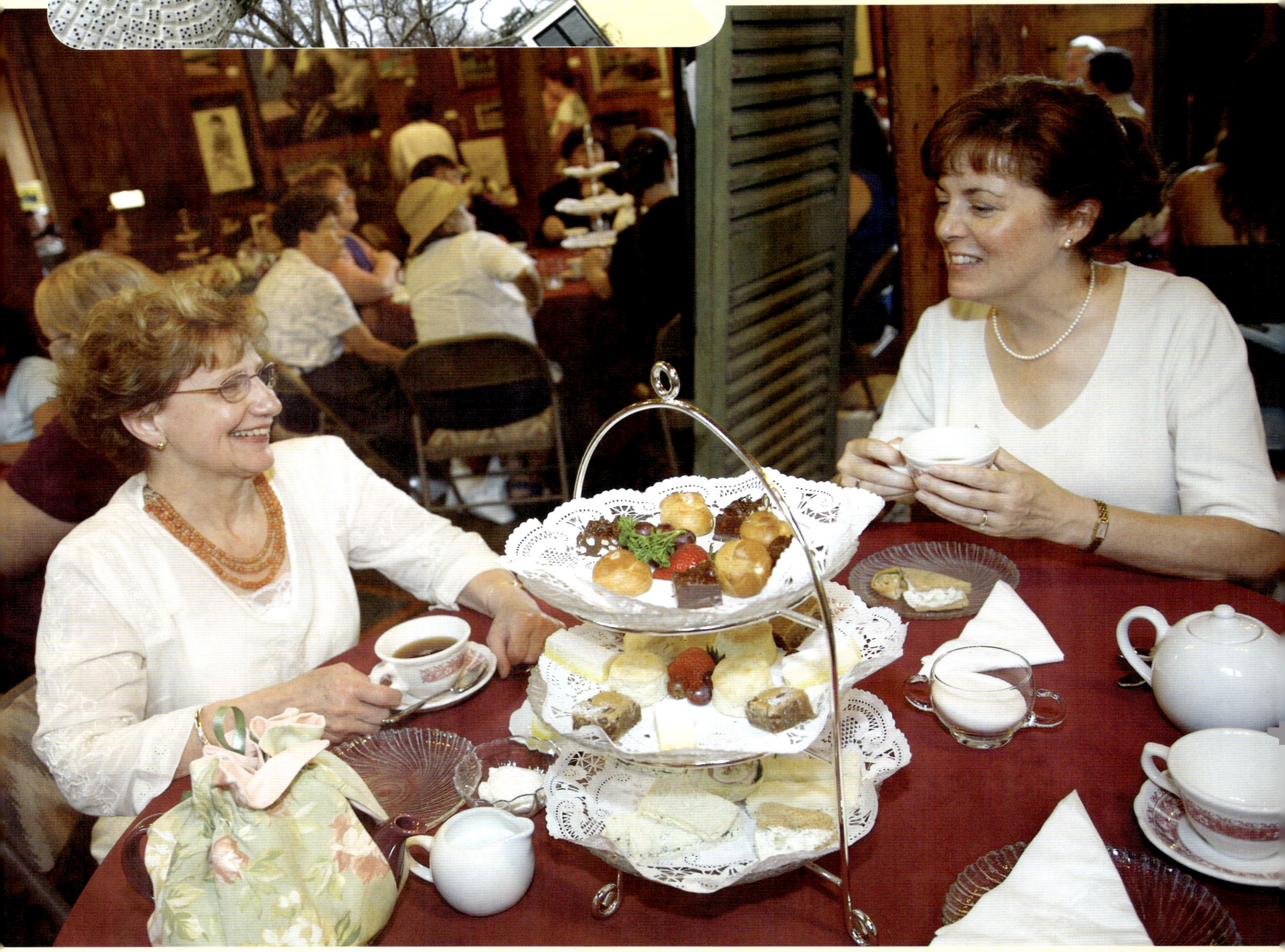

PHOTO BY JEANETTE BURKLE

Named for Loudoun County hero Francis Lightfoot Lee, whose signature appeared on the Declaration of Independence, the Lightfoot Restaurant in Leesburg is a delicious mélange of fine food, unusual atmosphere, and history. The restored 1888 building's first life was that of a bank. For more than half a century, citizens walked in and out of the facility then known as Peoples National Bank for financial transactions. In 1992, sisters Ingrid and Carrie Gustavson opened a small restaurant called the Lightfoot Café, which soon outgrew its sixty-seat capacity. The sisters renovated the Peoples National Bank in 1999, and today citizens come in not for an exchange of money, but for an exchange of good conversation and good food.

Loudoun County – A Photographic Portrait

PHOTO BY ALAN S. WEINER

Little Signy Roberts, with mom, Kay, doesn't know it yet, but even at this early age she's part of a beloved Delaplane tradition. Begun at the turn of the twentieth century, the Delaplane Strawberry Festival was fully revived by its citizens in 1976 and has been going strong ever since. Sponsored by the Emmanuel Episcopal Church, Piedmont Parish, the event is held on Saturday and Sunday each Memorial Day. Children's games, a car show, petting zoo, crafts shows, bake sales, live entertainment, and strawberry pie and jam contests are just a few of the fun activities. In 2006, the festival also hosted the first-ever National Strawberry Eating Championship.

PHOTO BY ALAN S. WEINER

PHOTO BY THOMAS S. ENGLAND

Golf ... Scottish Links Style

Everyone is a member for the day at this acclaimed golf course

With its dramatic rolling terrain, meandering streams, native hardwoods, and spectacular vistas, Raspberry Falls Golf & Hunt Club pays homage to its heritage as a history-rich northern Virginia plantation. Although it has the look, feel, and play of a premiere country club, the real beauty of the Gary Player–designed course is that it is an upscale daily fee course, open to all. The first to offer the "Member for the Day" experience, it continues to draw rave reviews from industry publications, the general media, and most importantly, golfers.

Developed by the firm of Stradinger and Swiger, Raspberry Falls Golf & Hunt Club officially opened in 1996 as an unusual blend of equestrians and golfers, of hooves and clubs. Once prime foxhunting lands, the local Loudoun Hunt West encouraged Bob Swiger, managing partner of Stradinger and Swiger, to allow the club to continue to hunt on the land. As a lover of history and tradition, Swiger agreed, designing a series of trails that traversed, but did not interfere with the course. Though there is no longer hunting on the land, the spirit of the hunt remains at Raspberry Falls.

As a number of new courses have opened and continue to open around the Washington metro area, Raspberry Falls—Gary Player's only signature course in Virginia—remains the standard by which other courses are judged. The first-class architecture and design of Raspberry Falls' 7,191-yard, par-72 layout is modeled in the Scottish links style. In the words of Gary Player, "Few Americans will have seen the kind of stacked-sod bunkers they find here, inspired as they are by the great seaside courses of the British Isles."

Along with its exceptional golf, outstanding customer service is another tradition on which the club has built its reputation. Honored in the Top 50 in the US in Customer Service by *Golf Digest*, golfers are greeted at the brass rail bag drop by cart attendants wearing hunt-red vests and black bow ties. "It is important to us that our golfers have a great experience from the time they drive up to our bag drop to the time they leave," said Bob Swiger.

With its exemplary design and outstanding customer service, it's no wonder that Raspberry Falls continues to receive many accolades from national and regional sources, including Top 10 Public or Private in Virginia (*Golf Digest*), Top 10 in the Mid-Atlantic (*Washington Golf Monthly*), Best Public Course (*Washington Times*), and Four Stars (*Golf Digest/Places to Play*).

"We look at our plaques and awards and are humbled and extremely grateful," says Swiger. While hundreds of thousands of rounds have been played on Raspberry Falls over the years, Swiger is not content to rest on the club's laurels. "Our challenge is to keep offering the best golf experience and to keep Raspberry Falls on our guests' must-play list." ✦

"Few Americans will have seen the kind of stacked-sod bunkers they find here, inspired as they are by the great seaside courses of the British Isles."

Raspberry Falls is an outstanding Gary Player design that nudges up to the foothills of the Blue Ridge Mountains. It gets so close, in fact, that two tee shots are hit from mountainsides into the valley that most of the course plays through.

The tree-lined entrance leading to the plantation-style clubhouse has the feel of a private club. But Raspberry Falls, with its country-club southern hospitality service, is a public course allowing everyone to experience one of Old Dominion's best.

PHOTO BY THOMAS S. ENGLAND

PHOTO BY ALAN S. WEINER

Summer splashin' is spectacular at Algonkian Park, one of the nineteen public parks of the Northern Virginia Regional Park Authority, and one of six located in Loudoun County. One of the coolest spots in the park is Downpour!—an aquatic playground featuring twin 140-foot flume slides that end in a large swimming pool. For water fun that's a bit tamer, an interactive play pool offers just as wet an experience, as a huge bucket dumps six hundred gallons of water every three minutes. Little splashers and swimmers also enjoy the Tad Pool, because it's just the right size.

PHOTO BY ALAN S. WEINER

Charlie Taylor shows Haylee, seven, and Trulee, two, that milk does not come in a carton from the local supermarket, but from cows like Milkie, a permanent resident of the Loudoun Heritage Farm Museum. When Loudoun County was founded in 1757, most of the population made their living farming the land, and farming continued to be the primary occupation until 1945. In the intervening years, residents realized that the loss of farmland also meant the loss of farming history. So a group of volunteers—mostly farmers—decided to do something about that. Loudoun County purchased 357 acres, which is now Claude Moore Park. In 1998 the Loudoun Heritage Farm Museum, Inc. was formed. It is a facility of the county Department of Parks, Recreation, and Community Services. The museum specializes in hands-on classes and programs that meet the Standards of Learning for Virginia.

PHOTO BY SCOTT INDERMAUR

When the locals are in the mood for a little fun on the water, they head over to Butts Tubes, a family-owned company that specializes in trips on the Shenandoah and Potomac rivers. Started as a low-cost tubing operation, Butts quickly grew its services to include trips using rafts, inflatable kayaks, and canoes. Today, whether it's a fast-moving whitewater rafting trip or a relaxing flatwater canoe ride, Butts offers an adventure to suit every member of the family.

PHOTO BY SCOTT INDERMAUR

United ... Today's Global Airline

Connecting you to more than 210 destinations worldwide

United Airlines has a long and distinguished history in aviation in this country and a long and mutually beneficial history with Dulles International Airport and Loudoun County.

United has been serving Loudoun and the Washington area for more than sixty years. In 1986, the airline began hub operations at Dulles, and four years later selected Dulles as its East Coast transatlantic gateway. Today, with key global air rights in the Asia-Pacific region, Europe, and Latin America, United is one of the largest international carriers based in the United States. To be more specific, the company operates more than thirty-seven hundred flights a day on United, United Express, and Ted to more than 210 domestic and international destinations from its hubs in Washington, D.C., Chicago, Denver, Los Angeles, and San Francisco. Locally, when United introduced the Boeing 777—recognized as the most technologically advanced airplane in the world—the company choose Dulles for the world inaugural.

Few passengers who stretch out and relax in air-conditioned comfort on United flights today know what early passengers endured. After World War I ended in 1918, the U.S. government found an important peacetime role for aviation: delivering mail. Several years later, commercial air transportation began on April 6, 1926. Walter T. Varney launched air mail service between Pasco, Washington, and Elko, Nevada. Because Varney's service was a predecessor of United, it also marked the birth of United Airlines.

Pilot Karl Minter, one of the leaders of United's Black Airline Pilots and the Aviation Core Enrichment Program (ACE), and pilot Gene Scanlon go through their aircraft check before a flight.

Early travelers who chose this new mode of transportation were an adventurous lot. They sat on mail sacks in cramped cabins, with neither heat in winter nor air conditioning in summer. The first flight attendants were nurses who served coffee and sandwiches and ministered to the comfort of apprehensive flyers. Air travel has come a long way.

United has also come a long way. Today, it is hard to imagine Loudoun County without Dulles Airport or the Loudoun community without United. In addition to the service it offers, United employs five thousand people who live in and contribute to the area, which, according to the Loudoun County Department of Economic Development, makes United Loudoun's fourth-largest employer.

"In an average year, more than 7 million passengers go through United's gates here. These passengers support local businesses, hotels, restaurants, museums, and the arts. In addition, we do business with approximately 160 different vendors, so you can see the extent to which we have an impact on the local economy," said Henry Bird, United's business manager at Dulles Airport.

Numbers and statistics tell part, but not all, of the story. United is very much involved in the immediate community. United has held a board position on the Loudoun Chamber of Commerce for at least ten years, and local representatives sit on a variety of other nonprofit boards.

continued on page 176

United has been serving Loudoun and the Washington area for more than sixty years.

Happy travelers Sonia and Philip Marshall board a United flight to the West Coast with friendly assistance from customer service agent Gloria Baysaer.

PHOTO BY SCOTT INDERMAUR

Architect Eero Saarinen designed the slope of the windows in the lobby of Dulles Airport to give the impression of flight. The sunlit space is an impressive background for United's Ticket Counter/Easy Check-In machines.

PHOTO BY SCOTT INDERMAUR

continued from page 175

Pilots and flight attendants also work hand-in-hand with the community. "We have a very strong civic interaction," said Captain Walt Clark, chief pilot. Nationally United is committed to the communities it serves. While the support takes many forms, it has a single goal: "to make the world a better place for our customers and employees to live, work, travel, and do business."

One of the areas in which United "helps the human spirit take flight" is in the support of organizations that address the needs of at-risk youth. "A good example is United's Organization of Black Airline Pilots," said Clark. "Each year they sponsor Aviation Core Enrichment (ACE) Camps, where youth are introduced to all the different elements of aviation and given a behind-the-scenes look at the profession.

"We also maintain a speakers bureau and frequently send pilots and flight attendants out to schools to speak to students and stress the importance of staying in school and staying out of trouble."

With 321 daily departures, United's mainline aircraft, United Express, and Ted serve Washington Dulles, United's East Coast hub. The cranes in the background are part of the expansion at Dulles, designed to accommodate the area's growth and the increased demand for air travel.

PHOTO BY SCOTT INDERMAUR

1K member Vincent Briones takes a moment to relax and make a phone call in one of United's spacious Red Carpet Clubs.

PHOTO BY SCOTT INDERMAUR

On a lighter note, United is also a Gold Sponsor for the Loudoun Summer Music Fest, which provides a fun and affordable, family-friendly concert atmosphere with entertainment from early June through the middle of August. United also charters the Redskins football team, which makes its home in Loudoun County.

In the 1920s, Pacific Air Transport flew between Los Angeles and Seattle. That company became the predecessor that evolved into today's global airline, United. Who could have guessed the impact that early flight along the West Coast would eventually have on Loudoun County? ✦

PHOTO BY SCOTT INDERMAUR

New flight attendant Ronada Hinton serves refreshments to customers enjoying the comfort of United's Economy Plus seating aboard a B-777.

Two of Loudoun County's most dedicated community activists, Major General Joseph T. Anderson (Ret.) and president and CEO of Bridgman Communications, Georgia Graves, standing by the Shuttle Enterprise at the National Air and Space Museum (NASM). As the museum's associate director, General Anderson created in the fall of 2005 a program that would serve as a thank-you to our nation's veterans recuperating at Walter Reed Army Medical Center and Bethesda Naval Hospital. The resulting "NASM on the Road" program consists of either a personal visit and virtual laptop museum tour or an on-site guided tour. These group visits—which include a tour of the museum's highlights, a ticket to the IMAX movie of their choice, lunch at the on-site McDonald's, and a visit with General Anderson— are a great way for veterans to spend quality time out of the hospital. "I think it's important to shake each of their hands, look them in the eye, and personally thank them for their service," he says. When not busy guiding her successful business, Graves also helps out with various community causes, and is a major fund-raiser for NASM on the Road. "She's one of the most active people I've seen in terms of civic action," says General Anderson. "If you want something done, just give Georgia a call."

Some people collect stamps, others salt and pepper shakers. Viola Townsend Winmill collected carriages—the horse-drawn kind. In 1928 she received her first as a birthday gift from her husband Robert. Viola drove her four-in-hand coach with her Welsh ponies to hunt races, meets, and Sunday luncheon parties. When she traveled abroad or in the United States, she often brought back another carriage until her collection grew to be more than 120 vehicles. Concern for the future of her carriages prompted the development of the Winmill Carriage Museum to "make sure I have an established place for the carriage collection when I die, so they aren't loosed all over the country, and are kept in Virginia if possible." The wish became reality in April 1970, just five years before her passing. The museum at Morven Park displays these cherished antique vehicles, including the first rotary motor Silsby Steamer Pumper, and the Sprinkler Wagon, used to keep the dust down in the city streets.

PHOTO BY THOMAS S. ENGLAND

Although located only minutes from one of the nation's busiest urban areas, Loudoun County also comprises vast expanses of rural areas—over 160,000 acres in total. So if your idea of the perfect place to live is tucked away on untouched acreage where the nearest neighbor is a long walk down a country lane away, you'll be sure to find it here.

Sparkling clean cars make for happy drivers and also make wishes come true for children. As the neighborhood car wash, Ashburn Car Wash enthusiastically supports community charities, like the Make-A-Wish Foundation, by donating a portion of the proceeds from every car washed on an annually designated day. The good neighbor also helps underwrite the fund-raising and the fun-generating events of local schools and youth sports.

PHOTO BY BRUCE R. FEELEY

Meeting Consumer Needs

Car wash provides squeaky-clean customer service

Superior service: Thompson Hospitality's reputation is built on this principle. Founded in 1992 by Warren M. Thompson, the company based in Herndon is the largest minority-owned food service business in the United States, operating proprietary restaurants and contracting food service. Thompson Hospitality also owns and operates Ashburn Car Wash in Loudoun County.

The leap from food service to a car wash isn't as broad as one might think, considering successful modern car washes are all about satisfying a consumer service need. "One of Thompson Hospitality's core values is customer service," says Benita Thompson-Byas, vice president for the family-owned business. "Whether it's a student who comes in the line for a meal at one of our universities; a diner visiting Obi Sushi, our restaurant at the Reston Town Center; or someone bringing their car in for a wash, what keeps people coming back is a high-quality product and great customer service," she says.

"What keeps people coming back is a high-quality product and great customer service."

Ashburn Car Wash is a neighborhood car wash, but it provides far more than a simple wash and dry. Services include three exterior wash packages and two interior packages, ranging from a basic wash to an ultimate detailing service. Better than a hand wash, they use brushless computer-driven equipment, softer water, and specially formulated and environmentally friendly shampoos; what's more, 85 percent of the water is recycled. But most of all, Ashburn Car Wash guarantees that if the customer is not satisfied with the wash for any reason (or if it rains within twenty-four hours of the wash), they will re-wash it for free. Now that's superior service! ✦

PHOTO BY ANN HIGGINS

Ian DeHaven visits with a draft horse at Ayrshire Farm during the Loudoun Spring Farm Tour. Twice each year the Department of Economic Development organizes free, self-guided tours of dozens of the county's innovative niche farms. The tours attract thousands of visitors from as far away as the West Coast, and allow families the chance to visit with farm animals; select fruits, vegetables, and trees direct from the fields; tour wineries; and buy high-quality, local farm products.

PHOTO BY JEANETTE BURKLE

PHOTO BY JEANETTE BURKLE

Each year for six days at the end of July, the Loudoun County Fair brings an old-time sense of fun to the area. In addition to livestock auctions, a professional rodeo, 4-H animal projects, and crafts exhibits, there's a midway for the young and young at heart, musical entertainment, and, of course, plenty of fair food staples—enough cotton candy, hot dogs, and turkey legs to keep the kids happy and the adults happily off their diets.

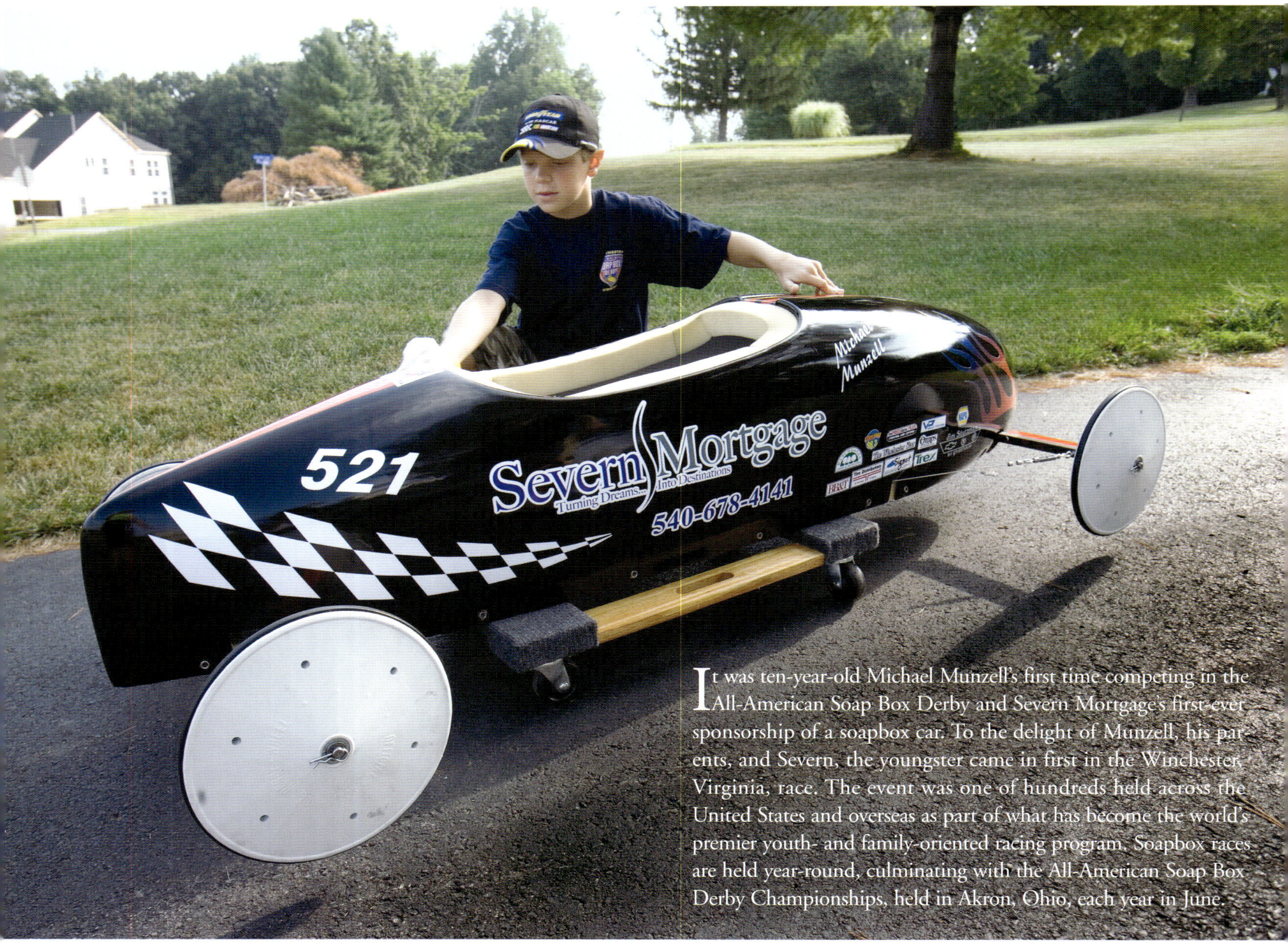

It was ten-year-old Michael Munzell's first time competing in the All-American Soap Box Derby and Severn Mortgage's first-ever sponsorship of a soapbox car. To the delight of Munzell, his parents, and Severn, the youngster came in first in the Winchester, Virginia, race. The event was one of hundreds held across the United States and overseas as part of what has become the world's premier youth- and family-oriented racing program. Soapbox races are held year-round, culminating with the All-American Soap Box Derby Championships, held in Akron, Ohio, each year in June.

PHOTO BY SCOTT INDERMAUR

Combining their passion for softball with the desire to give back has spurred Severn Mortgage to support and sponsor many area softball teams in Loudoun County over the years. Most recently, they sponsored the Round Hill Mustangs, a ULGSL 12U Girls Fastpitch Softball team, not only with donations but with volunteer time, with Lawrie Vick, president of Severn Mortgage, serving as coach. Their 2006 season ended with winning the tournament in their age bracket and becoming 2006 season champions. Go Stangs!

PHOTO BY DAVE GALEN

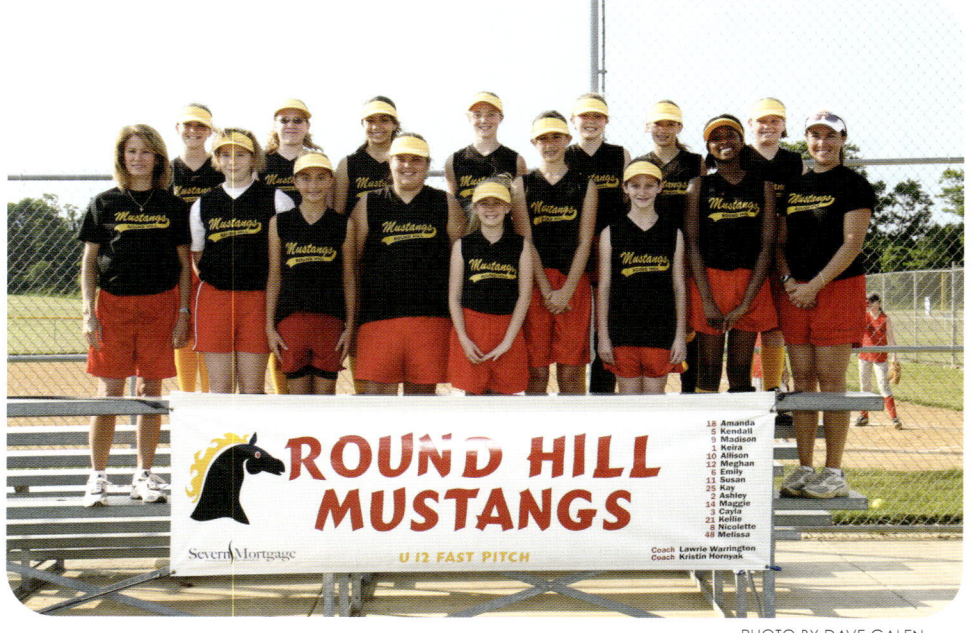

Yㅇu can hear them rumbling through town, the hundreds of bikers with a purpose. The America's 9-11 Memorial Ride, honoring our country's first responders, begins in Pennsylvania, heads to the Pentagon, and ends in New York City. The route brings the ride through downtown Leesburg, a popular spot for parades and ceremonies to honor the important events of our country's history.

PHOTO BY SCOTT INDERMAUR

PHOTO BY BRUCE R. FEELEY

Ambience Leaves Lasting Impression

Hotel blends historic charm with modern convenience

What's strikingly different about the Holiday Inn at Historic Carrodoc Hall is the stately eighteenth-century mansion that is the centerpiece of the property. Originally known as Oak Grove, the home stands today as it did when constructed in 1747. The front brickwork, done in "English Flemish Bond" like so many other buildings of the period, reaches like open arms to welcome visitors inside. By combining historic charm with today's necessary conveniences, the hotel assures that business and leisure travelers experience a unique stay that is both pleasurable and productive.

Located on Route 7 in historic Leesburg and standing on land graced by grand old trees and natural springs, the hotel feels worlds away from the hustle of the city. Yet, Dulles International Airport is a short fourteen-mile drive by complimentary shuttle service or by personal car. Other points of interest in the northern Virginia/Washington, D.C., area are no further than thirty-five miles. The hotel's convenient location makes it attractive to business travelers and leisure travelers alike. In addition, the 5,477 square feet of flexible meeting space make it an attractive location for corporate and social functions.

The Holiday Inn at Historic Carrodoc Hall features 126 guest rooms with standard amenities for comfort, convenience, and productivity, including cable television, complimentary high-speed wireless Internet access, two-line telephones with voice mail, an executive work station with a data port, and the usual morning wake-up essentials like alarm clock/radio, coffeemaker, hairdryer, and weekday paper. By request, feather pillows, in-room refrigerators, and microwaves are available. In addition, as a full-service hotel, the Holiday Inn offers a fitness center, seasonal outdoor pool, self-serve guest laundry area, and business center, as well as complimentary on-site parking.

The heart of the hotel, however, is the lovely mansion that is akin to a bed and breakfast, with its Mansion House Restaurant on the main floor and four elegantly restored guest suites upstairs. Often requested for special occasions, the suites have a living area separated from the bedroom. "They're perfect for people looking for a historical weekend getaway," says Judy McHenry, sales director. "Each one is different and decorated in the period—like a B&B with the conveniences of a modern hotel." A similar atmosphere prevails in the Mansion House Restaurant. Featuring hand-crafted furniture and two cozy fireplaces, the restaurant serves guests steaks, seafood, and poultry, and a full Sunday brunch that regularly draws a local crowd as well.

continued on page 190

By combining historic charm with today's necessary conveniences, the hotel assures that travelers experience a unique stay that is both pleasurable and productive.

Attached to the 1747 Historic Carrodoc Hall, which includes the Mansion House Restaurant and four unique guest suites, this hotel is a full-service Holiday Inn that includes 122 guest rooms.

The Mansion House Restaurant offers cozy hearthside dining.

PHOTO BY ALAN S. WEINER

The unique guestrooms offer a B&B feel with the conveniences of a full-service hotel.

PHOTO BY ALAN S. WEINER

continued from page 189

The distinctive ambience of the Holiday Inn at Historic Carrodoc Hall is just one of the reasons this hotel property leaves a lasting impression on guests. Customer service is another. For the staff at the hotel, "going the extra mile" is second nature. Many of the employees are longtime residents of the area and are eager to share insider's knowledge of the nooks and crannies of Loudoun County and its surroundings. "We realize that visitors have a lot of choices, so we set ourselves apart not just in the uniqueness of our property, but in our service to our customers." ✦

The perfect location for meetings or social events, the Holiday Inn Leesburg offers five banquet rooms, seating up to three hundred people.

PHOTO BY ALAN S. WEINER

There's apple pie, and then there's Mom's Apple Pie. With fresh-peeled fruit right off the trees in the Shenandoah Valley, the pies made by this fourth-generation family-owned and -operated bakery are as close to Mother's best as any pie can be. Customers like Pat Burhans of Charleston, West Virginia, say they can savor the fruits of Mom's labor in the pies because Mom's Apple Pie deliberately adds sugar sparingly. Although the all-American dessert got this business started, the bakery is also famous for many other sweet treats, like Virginia blackberry pie, bourbon walnut pie, lemon chess pie, as well as half-hearted (as in shaped) cookies, and gingerbread boys and girls.

PHOTO BY THOMAS S. ENGLAND

PHOTO BY SCOTT INDERMAUR

Walking through Oatlands Plantation is truly taking a walk through history. Oatlands was established in 1798 from 3,408 acres of prime Loudoun County farmland. The owner, George Carter, based his economy on wheat production. He soon added other small grains, raised sheep, planted a vineyard, and built a mill complex and a sawmill for timber. In 1804, he began building a classic Federal-style mansion, which he later embellished with terraced gardens, a propagation greenhouse, a smokehouse, and a three-story barn. When he died, his widow Elizabeth Grayson Carter stayed at Oatlands and managed the property through the Civil War. Failing fortunes caused George Jr. and his wife to operate Oatlands first as a girls' school and later as a summer boarding house. In 1897, Stilson Hutchins, founder of the *Washington Post*, bought the mansion and sixty acres. Less than ten years later the property was sold to William and Edith Eustis. He was an avid equestrian, and she was an equally talented gardener. In 1964, their daughters donated the mansion, its furnishings, and 261 surrounding acres to the National Trust for Historic Preservation. Today Oatlands has four seasons of activities that make it self-supporting. Afternoon tea is a highlight of any visit to Oatlands.

Quality of Life ... A Question of Balance

An authentic hometown in one of the nation's fastest-growing counties

The town resides comfortably between history and progress, between mountain foothills and metropolitan bustle . . . at the intersection of Virginia's historic Alexandria and Carolina roads. The town is Leesburg, Virginia, and since 1758, it has been at the crossroads of all things important, while preserving its legacy as an authentic hometown where business, family life, and tourism intersect to create an enviable quality of life.

Today, as the seat of government for one of the country's fastest-growing counties, Leesburg embraces the advantages of being close to the nation's capital while safeguarding the small-town character that defines it. Despite its phenomenal growth over the past decade, Leesburg remains a place where neighbors rub elbows at the local coffee shop or grocery and share thoughts about the events of their daily lives. Yet, with direct access to the Washington Dulles International Airport and the Capital Beltway via the Dulles Greenway toll road, residents are only twenty minutes from the airport and less than an hour from downtown Washington, D.C. In addition, Leesburg Executive Airport, one of the region's busiest general aviation airports, provides advantages as a corporate location unparalleled in the greater Washington, D.C., metro area. Clearly, Leesburg offers the proverbial best of both worlds: close enough for convenience, yet removed enough for a quiet, simpler life.

In Leesburg, character and family values count as much as growth and progress. It's a community that invests in the long term, not just through educating the future workforce with high-ranking public schools, but also through its desire and ability to attract quality businesses and employees. The historic and charming downtown of Leesburg is a draw for

PHOTO BY JEANETTE BURKLE

Leesburg's fire department dates back to the 1800s, when citizens formed a bucket brigade known as the Star Company. In 1863, the group organized and changed its name to the Leesburg Fire Company.

PHOTO BY SCOTT INDERMAUR

photographers, history buffs, and tourists alike. The picturesque mix of historic buildings, specialty retail shops, restaurants, and local government offices combines to create a fertile business environment and intensifying arts community. Proximity to Washington, D.C., Maryland's Biotech Corridor, and northern Virginia's high-tech sector provides significant opportunities for sustainable business growth. Addressing the Town's Legacy Businesses at the annual Business Appreciation Awards Ceremony, the Honorable Kristen C. Umstattd, mayor of Leesburg, said that "Leesburg is home to a diverse business community that truly makes it possible to live, work in, and enjoy the Town." She went on to state, "The Town is committed to strongly supporting its business community, whether by fostering entrepreneurial development, taking proactive stances on development issues like broadband access within the Town, or working to streamline its land-use development review process."

The right balance of work and play is essential to a community's optimal quality of life. Once again, Leesburg is poised in the crossroads. Nestled in the foothills of the beautiful Blue Ridge Mountains, Leesburg's cultural and recreational amenities extend in many directions. In the downtown, walking tours tell tales dating back to Colonial times. The Town's Thomas Balch Library boasts one of the area's most extensive genealogy and local history collections. Parades—including the longest-running Halloween parade east of the Mississippi—delight the young and the young at heart.

Leesburg remains a place where neighbors rub elbows at the local coffee shop or grocery and share thoughts about the events of their daily lives.

The Fourth of July Celebration in Historic Downtown Leesburg is a classic community celebration. Families, neighbors, and friends gather to watch the parade during the day, and fireworks at Ida Lee Park in the evening.

continued on page 196

Historic Leesburg's fine art galleries, specialty shops, theatre, and restaurants offer a delightful evening out for residents and visitors on the First Friday of each month, February through December. Entertainment, festivity, and energy fill the air.

PHOTO BY DAVE GALEN

continued from page 195

Outdoor summer concerts and fall arts festivals are held in area parks and in the historic downtown. In addition, skate parks, bike trails, and other recreational amenities, including the recently expanded recreation center at Ida Lee Park and the athletic fields at Freedom Park, offer something for all levels of sport enthusiasts. The Washington & Old Dominion Trail provides connectivity with neighboring communities to the east and west of the town.

Just beyond Leesburg's borders, within a short, scenic drive from town, lie myriad rural delights, including bird watching at the Rust Audubon Sanctuary, golf on idyllic Scottish-inspired courses, steeplechase races at Morven Park,

Leesburg Executive Airport is well known as pilot friendly. Welcoming Gulfstreams and Cubs alike, Leesburg Executive Airport delivers comprehensive services without the congestion, expense, and delays common to larger airports. Whether flying into Leesburg Executive Airport for business or pleasure, you'll find experienced aviation professionals available to ensure that your plane and your plans are in good hands.

PHOTO BY THOMAS S. ENGLAND

Leesburg's Annual Flower and Garden Festival brings a rich combination of flora, plants, landscape architecture, and true artistry to the Historic Downtown area. Music and children's events complement the festival.

PHOTO BY BRUCE R. FEELEY

and hiking in the mountains. The cultural activities of the Capital District await those who venture in that direction, although Leesburg's cosmopolitan position is ever growing. Shopping is abundant in several directions, including Leesburg's Downtown Historic District, where unique stores thrive in attractively restored buildings. Shoppers also find edible items at the seasonal farmers market, antiques and collectibles throughout town, and quality bargains at the Leesburg Corner Premium Outlets at the town's eastern gateway.

Leesburg's rich character is rooted in the town's historic past. Leesburg is well positioned to continue its evolution as a diverse community in the future. According to Karen Jones, former chairman of Leesburg's Economic Development Commission, "Recognizing that Leesburg's continued growth as well as the growth in the surrounding parts of Loudoun County threatens to overwhelm the town's historic small-town character, our work on our comprehensive economic development plan, which includes preservation and tourism efforts, is critically important to retaining the town's charm and authenticity." ✦

Loudoun County High School recently celebrated fifty years of educating area students. The deep traditions are illustrated in the architecture of the building, the front lawn celebration, and the smiles of the talented graduates.

PHOTO BY THOMAS S. ENGLAND

Few joys in the world equal the exhilaration of being out of school for the summer. And what better way to celebrate than a party with friends at the Purcellville Skating Rink, complete with invitations, decorations, skate passes, table covers, and helium balloons? The original building, which could hold three thousand people and cost twenty-five hundred dollars to build, has a long and colorful history. Constructed in 1903, it has served a wide range of tenants, including Prohibition meetings, wrestling matches, a performance center, and Loudoun's first 4-H Fair. Today, the Purcellville—or P'ville as it's known to locals—Skating Rink is the place to hang out and have fun on wheels. Visitors can rent both inline or classic quad skates in sizes from juvenile eight to adult fourteen. The rink has programs for every age. Admission is free on Teen Center Friday Nights, and the music rocks. Tuesday and Wednesday mornings are Open Toddler Time. Parents are encouraged to bring along children's toys such as balls or push-and-ride toys. The music is kid-friendly, and the colored lights add to the party atmosphere.

PHOTO BY THOMAS S. ENGLAND

PHOTO BY SCOTT INDERMAUR

For Jeremiah Twieg of Hagerstown, Maryland, bicycling isn't a leisure sport. In fact, his wheels barely ever touch the ground, at least not both at once. For him the point is to move as quickly and jump as high as possible while charging over ramps and dodging various obstacles at Catoctin Skate Park. Here, like-minded bicyclists, skateboarders, and in-line skaters can test their skill on the park's smooth asphalt-coated skating surface that's dotted with a variety of launch ramps, fun boxes, rail slides, and half-pipes. The facility was developed through a unique collaborative effort between a group of young Leesburg skaters, the Town of Leesburg Parks and Recreation Department, and the Friends of Ida Lee, and included public and private financial support, in-kind donations, and grassroots fund-raising efforts. Located at Ida Lee Park Recreation Center, Catoctin Skate Park is open year-round, seven days a week, and admission is free.

One of the best ways to enjoy Loudoun County's rural beauty is with a tour through its back roads. A popular route runs along the Snickersville Turnpike, a famous nineteenth-century road that was used by both the Union and the Confederacy to move their troops. Today the Turnpike is one of Loudoun County's seven Virginia Byways, which were adopted by the General Assembly in 1988. Linking some of the area's oldest villages as well as numerous recreational, cultural, and historical sites, the Snickersville Turnpike starts on Route 50 at Aldie, travels northwest over Goose Creek and through Bluemont, climbs to 950 feet, and meets Route 7 where it crosses the Blue Ridge Mountains through Snickers' Gap. The byway is maintained by the Snickersville Turnpike Association, a group of local residents who ensure road maintenance and safety while at the same time preserving the route's historic and aesthetic beauty, including many old stone walls, stone bridges, and centuries-old trees.

An American Success Story

They are in the driver's seat

It has all the elements of a Horatio Alger novel. A young man with courage and fortitude achieves success against all odds. The man is William Bouweiri, who came to America from Lebanon, learned English, and got a job driving a limousine. One day a client was so impressed with Bouweiri's tour of Washington, D.C., that she paid her $179.50 fare and gave him a $5,000 tip. Bouweiri used the money to buy his first limousine, and Reston Limousine was on its way.

Two years later, he met Kristina. She was born in Japan, and her parents, who worked for the Foreign Service, had lived all over the world. In 1991 William and Kristina married and began a ten-year partnership in the business.

"We worked very hard," said Kristina, "but we were also very lucky. One day a man came and asked if we had a bus that wouldn't break down. We did, and that resulted in our first government contract." Currently they have 135 vehicles serving government agencies, universities, embassies, airports, and hospitals in Virginia, Washington, D.C., and Maryland. "We are the largest limo service in Virginia and Washington, and we're fully licensed. That's important because we can legally transport customers throughout the tri-state area. To protect our customers, we carry $5 million in insurance. We also have small cameras installed in each vehicle. We download the information daily, and our safety manager reviews it with our drivers."

PHOTO BY SCOTT INDERMAUR

In addition to superior service, the Reston Limousine fleet offers clients a lot more than just limousines. Clients can select a sedan, limo, Hummer, coach bus, Vanterra, or SUV. Each vehicle is driven by a licensed chauffeur, stylishly dressed in a black suit and white shirt, and trained to deliver exemplary service. Clients have confidence in Reston because this company definitely knows its way around.

PHOTO BY SCOTT INDERMAUR

Husband-and-wife team Kristina and William Bouweiri, owners of Reston Limousine Service, Inc., have recently opened their new twenty-thousand-square-foot, state-of-the-art facility near Dulles Town Center Mall. The building has full maintenance for their fleet of 135 vehicles, which includes sedans, vans, limos, and buses. The building also houses office space for the staff.

This success story does not end with William. After working together for a decade, the Bouweiris decided to build a home in Loudoun County for their growing family of four children. William stayed home to supervise the process. "After three months, we realized our business was running smoother with just one decision-maker in the office. William is still chairman of the company, but as president and CEO I run things day-to-day and consult him on major issues. It's nontraditional, but it works for us," Kristina said. She has been officially recognized for her community and corporate accomplishments.

In 2001, Reston bought land near Dulles Airport and constructed a custom-built facility with office space, one hundred parking spaces, five maintenance bays, and a staff of mechanics available 24/7. "We plan to offer maintenance to hotel vans in the Loudoun County area. Currently that service isn't available locally."

Another service is Reston Limousine's wine tours, which run every weekend. "We frequently give nonprofits free passes to use as door prizes. It's a good way to promote the Virginia wine industry and tourism in the area," said Kristina.

Reston supports a number of local charities, including the Make-A-Wish Foundation, the Children's Inn at the National Institute of Health, the Juvenile Diabetes Foundation, and the International Children's Arts Festival.

"Our name may reflect the town where William started the business, but we live and work in Loudoun County." And that's where the dream continues. ✦

"Our name may reflect the town where William started the business, but we live and work in Loudoun County."

A ttached to the 1747 Historic Carrodoc Hall, which includes the Mansion House Restaurant and four unique guest suites, this hotel is a full-service Holiday Inn that includes 122 guest rooms also located on the property.

PHOTO BY BRUCE R. FEELEY

No doubt the perfect getaway for couples and families, the Lansdowne resort also offers exclusive golf, dining, and spa membership packages for local residents and businesses, allowing them to enjoy the best of the resort at very special prices. Through its Resort Rewards travel and hospitality program, executives of member companies are also eligible for special rates, services, and amenities. Left: Playing golf for a good cause is a great way to support the community. American Home Mortgage was the 10K Hole-in-One Sponsor of the Fourteenth Annual Dulles Area Association of REALTORS' (DAAR) Golf Tournament at the River Creek Country Club in Leesburg. In addition to players and sponsors, the weather cooperated by providing a perfect day for the event. DAAR donated four thousand dollars from the tournament to Loudoun County Habitat for Humanity.

Things are always growing and improving at the five-hundred-acre Windham Winery, and a recent major shift was changing its name to Doukenie Winery. Doukenie—which means duchess—was the surname of the family matriarch, who came to America from Greece. Today her daughter Hope, and her grandson Dr. George Bazaco and his wife Nicki, run the winery. Doukenie offers nine wines, eight of them award-winners. Nicki, who is generally in charge of hospitality at special events, displays the head of a roast pig at a Father's Day BBQ. The winery regularly hosts three major events a year: the Taste of Greece in the spring, the Taste of Italy in the fall, and a Taste of the Holidays in December. The first vines at the winery were planted in 1985, and there are now ten acres planted and producing. "We may not produce the most wine in Virginia, but we try to produce the best," said Dr. Bazaco.

"A loaf of bread, a jug of wine, and thou." On a warm day, what better way to enjoy the outdoors than with a picnic? Tom Grant and Laurie Fyock decided to do just that down by the pond at the Doukenie Winery. It has taken a while—the first wine-making in the area began in 1608—but Virginia wineries have finally come into their own. As recently as 1979, the state had only six wineries, but today Virginia is home to more than two hundred vineyards, one hundred wineries, and a vast array of award-winning vintages. More than five hundred thousand people visit Virginia's wine country each year. The state ranks tenth in commercial grape production in the United States. There are three major grape varieties: vinifera grapes used in Chardonnay, Pinot Grigio, Riesling, Sauvignon Blanc, Cabernet Sauvignon, Merlot, and Pinot Noir; hybrid grapes used in making Seyval, Vidal Blanc, and Chambourcin; and American indigenous grapes, which produce Concord, Delaware, Niagara, and Norton. Thomas Jefferson set out to convert colonists to wine from their whisky- and beer-drinking ways, and his efforts have finally borne fruit.

PHOTO BY THOMAS S. ENGLAND

Gracious Living Joins World-Class Service

Serenity plus cosmopolitan excitement at Creighton Farms

"TWO ROADS DIVERGED IN A WOODS, AND I

I TOOK THE ONE LESS TRAVELED BY

AND THAT HAS MADE ALL THE DIFFERENCE."

Robert Frost, *The Road Not Taken*

Taking the road less traveled in Loudoun County will bring you to The Ritz-Carlton Golf Club at Creighton Farms, a spectacular residential and country club community—and that indeed makes quite a bit of difference.

Local developer and homebuilder Creighton Enterprises had the vision to assemble a breathtaking property, while partnering with Juno Properties, LLC, The Ritz-Carlton, and Nicklaus Design to complete the picture. This panoramic property, just a breath away from the nation's capital, and the opportunity it presents to join forces in a significant effort were the catalysts uniting these distinguished leaders of their respective fields.

Combining the unique qualities of nationally recognized developer Juno Properties, LLC with The Ritz-Carlton's benchmark for service and a Jack Nicklaus Signature Design Golf Course, resident and nonresident members enjoy the best of luxury estate living, world-class service, and legendary golf and country club amenities.

Situated on more than nine hundred acres between the historic and picturesque towns of Leesburg and Middleburg, yet within easy access to Dulles International Airport and Washington, D.C., Creighton Farms is a unique combination of country serenity and cosmopolitan excitement.

The property's limited number of three- to six-acre home sites afford dramatic views of the countryside's rolling beauty, the Blue Ridge Mountains, and an exceptional golf course destined for recognition throughout the mid-Atlantic region. Custom-built homes, each in carefully planned settings, are the products of selected master craftspeople using only the highest-quality materials.

Adding a special quality to the community is the acclaimed concierge services of The Ritz-Carlton—now available to the homeowners at Creighton Farms. The personal needs of residents are anticipated and met through the stellar services provided by an on-site staff, adding to the gracious lifestyle that Creighton Farms inspires.

continued on page 210

The Club's mission is to ensure an experience that enlivens the senses and instills a sense of well-being, while exceeding the wishes and needs of members and residents.

Father and son enjoy a day of steeplechase racing with guests at The Ritz-Carlton Creighton Farms' sponsor tent at the Virginia Gold Cup.

Loudoun County's rolling terrain offers the perfect positioning for The Ritz-Carlton Golf Club's 475-yard par-4 Hole number 4. The course is designed to offer a challenge to golfers of all levels.

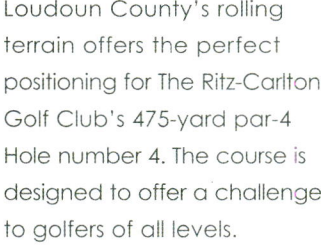

Golfing legend Jack Nicklaus (right) walks the course during one of his many construction reviews of his new Signature Design course at Creighton Farms.

continued from page 209

The development is the first in an exclusive agreement between Juno Properties, LLC, Nicklaus Design and The Ritz-Carlton. Juno Properties proudly views Creighton Farms as an opportunity to make a long-term commitment of active involvement in the Loudoun community, while at the same time serving as good stewards of the land.

In terms of land protection and preservation, The Ritz-Carlton has been recognized by Audubon International as a Certified Audubon Cooperative Sanctuary for its outstanding work at The Ritz-Carlton Golf Club & Spa in Jupiter, Florida. The same best management practices that achieved this award are being applied to protecting the wildlife-friendly environment at Creighton Farms.

"What stood out when we initially surveyed the property was the beauty of the valley, the trees, and the wetlands," says Jack Nicklaus. He adds, "The golf course is designed to play off nature, to work around and over the wetlands, to fit the land so that it is totally different from anything, anywhere else."

The course places a premium on strategy and precision rather than power and offers golfers of all levels a challenge. "We have taken advantage of a site with rolling terrain and some very appealing water features," says Nicklaus, who adds that "on more than one hole, players contend with

The natural beauty of the landscape enhances each vista from The Ritz-Carlton Golf Club at Creighton Farms.

It's early morning, the air is crisp and clear and Hole number 6, a 150-yard par-3, is ready and waiting. "The golf course is designed to play off nature, to work around and over the wetlands, to fit the land so that it is totally different from anything, anywhere else," Jack Nicklaus comments.

At The Ritz-Carlton Golf Club, Hole number 7, a 590-yard par-5, rests among the splendor of mature trees and breathtaking scenery. Jack Nicklaus says, "What stood out when we initially surveyed the property was the beauty of the valley, the trees, and the wetlands."

a small, but richly foliaged creek that meanders through the property." Nicklaus has been intimately involved with the project from its beginning, frequently returning to oversee the course development.

The Ritz-Carlton Golf Club at Creighton Farms provides the finest personal service and facilities for families and members who find a warm, relaxed, yet refined ambience. The Club's mission is to ensure an experience that enlivens the senses and instills a sense of well-being, while exceeding the wishes and needs of members and residents.

The center of community life for families is The Clubhouse. In addition to superb dining, The Club offers everything from a fitness studio to guided nature tours and a wealth of activities and programs, including Ritz Kids events, particular favorites for youngsters. As part of its commitment to the environment, Creighton Farms provides educational opportunities for adults to learn about native plants, birds, and animals who share the community, while encouraging younger members to take part in ecological activities for an early start toward an appreciation of nature.

Resident families of Creighton Farms and members of The Ritz-Carlton Golf Club find that choosing the road less traveled does truly make all the difference. ✦

Kris and Donald Jewell of Sterling, Virginia, enjoy a meal together at the Eiffel Tower Café. Located in the heart of Leesburg, this charming eatery offers authentic French cuisine in an inviting atmosphere. The café is owned and operated by Paris native Madeleine Sosnitsky, whose resumé includes an impressive eleven-year stint at Washington's renowned Sans Souci restaurant. The Eiffel Tower has been touted in Washington publications for its cuisine as well as its ambience, which on weekends often includes a musical serenade. With a seasonal menu that features seafood dishes and artistic desserts, the Eiffel Tower offers something sure to please every taste.

PHOTO BY SCOTT INDERMAUR

PHOTO BY ALAN S. WEINER

Dinner in the restaurant located at Patowmack Farm is so much more than a meal. It's an experience that also incorporates wonderful sights, sounds, and smells. Diners are treated to spectacular nighttime views of the Potomac River while feasting on the venue's highly acclaimed modern European cuisine, which incorporates the farm's organic produce and free-range eggs, as well as organic and natural meats and fish from sustainable fisheries. Depending on the weather, seating is available inside the air-conditioned and heated glass conservatory or under an open-air tent. A working farm that specializes in a variety of fresh herbs, lettuces, vegetables, fruits, and squashes, Patowmack Farm was established in 1986 by owners Chuck and Beverly Billand as an expression of the couple's lifelong love of delicious, healthful food and the farming lifestyle.

PHOTO BY SCOTT INDERMAUR

The heart of Leesburg is the historic downtown. As the seat of government, it is the pivotal point for business, shopping, dining, and cultural events. Among its treasures are Loudoun Museum, Thomas Balch Library, Dodona Manor, and the historic County Courthouse.

PHOTO BY THOMAS S. ENGLAND

PHOTO BY THOMAS S. ENGLAND

Each year, thousands of people celebrate their Celtic heritage at the Potomac Celtic Festival, the largest event of its kind in the Mid-Atlantic. Held the second weekend of June at Leesburg's Morven Park International Equestrian Center, the Potomac Celtic Festival invites performers, craftspeople, and vendors from around the globe to celebrate the culture and heritage of the seven Celtic Nations of Ireland, Scotland, Wales, Isle of Man, Brittany, Galicia/Asturias, and Cornwall. The festivities kick off on Saturday morning with the procession of participating clans, followed by two days of crafts shows and demonstrations, a living history camp, Highland games, storytelling, and numerous children's activities. Music is of course an important part of the festival, and various bands play throughout the weekend. The highlight of the event, however, is NiteFest! which attracts to the main stage some of the world's best-known Celtic musical performers, augmented with plenty of great food, beer, and nonalcoholic beverages.

PHOTO BY THOMAS S. ENGLAND

PHOTO BY THOMAS S. ENGLAND

PHOTO BY THOMAS S. ENGLAND

A Family History of Excellence

Selling the best of American-made

When a client completes a purchase at Moore Cadillac Hummer, they're buying more than just an automobile. They're investing in a legacy of quality and performance.

"These are great American products, and we are proud to be able to represent them," says general manager Joe Moore. "Our people put our customers first, and it's our goal to provide them with an experience that goes beyond sales, and continues into service and support long after they leave the showroom floor."

The Moore family of dealerships was established in 1964 in York, Pennsylvania, by founder Joe Moore Sr. In 1978 the enterprising salesman opened Moore Cadillac in Tysons Corner, Virginia, today the most successful Cadillac dealership in the Washington, D.C., metropolitan area. Mr. Moore Sr. remains president of the company, while his grandson

Joe Moore serves as general manager of both Tysons Corner and the family's newest location at Chantilly, opened in 2005.

As the premier automotive showroom in the county, the Chantilly Moore Cadillac Hummer dealership represents a significant investment in Loudoun County. "Because of the tremendous growth and number of successful businesses in Loudoun County, we believe it's a great showcase for Cadillac and Hummer," continues Moore.

Between the two dealerships, Moore Cadillac Hummer employs over 250 managers, salespeople, and support staff. Together, they work to reflect the company's core philosophy of treating people with respect and courtesy, representing a stellar product, and providing accessible postsales service and support.

"We have very clear expectations for our people," says Moore. "We provide all our employees with thorough training, and we certify them on an annual basis. It's critical to our operation's success that everyone embodies our culture."

That ethic has resulted in consistently top sales figures since the Chantilly dealership's opening, as well as a high level of customer satisfaction. And for exemplary effort at both locations, Mr. Moore Sr. is the only dealer in the country named as a Cadillac Master Dealer every year since the award's inception.

continued on page 218

"These are great American products, and we are proud to be able to represent them."

Two luxury automobiles, two luxury showrooms! The company's 37,666-square-foot Cadillac dealership occupies two stories, and its Hummer dealership provides over 11,500 square feet of single-story showroom space. Together, the two buildings showcase more Cadillacs and Hummers than any other dealership in the state.

PHOTO BY THOMAS S. ENGLAND

PHOTO BY THOMAS S. ENGLAND

Hummer is one of the world's premier luxury vehicles, whose sturdiness was forged on years of military service. Buyers wanting to test the Hummer's prowess will soon get the chance to do so at the dealership's road-test course.

continued from page 217

Moore says the company's goals for the future are to continue as a resource of opportunity in Loudoun County. "Our number-one priority is to attract the best people, provide opportunities for them to grow professionally and personally, and to provide our customers with the best sales and service available." ✦

With its team of highly skilled specialists and all the latest factory paints, Moore Cadillac Hummer's Collision and Service Center can restore your vehicle to like-new condition. Its three-step repair process is simple: drop off, relax, and pick up. For its expert skill and service, the center was voted the number-one body shop in town by Channel 9 WUSA.

PHOTO BY THOMAS S. ENGLAND

Leesburg is the epicenter for historic research on Loudoun County. Founded in 1758, there's an almost infinite amount of the past to explore, including the Old Courthouse, the last of the three courthouses erected in the county, and the only one remaining. Part of the Leesburg Historic District recognized by the Virginia Landmarks Commission, the courthouse was erected in 1895. Although the statue of the Confederate soldier standing tall in front of the structure is a reminder of the many Rebel soldiers who gave their lives for the cause, everyday "battles for justice" carry on in the modern courthouse today, home to the Circuit Court of Loudoun County, and adjoined by other county offices and the Juvenile and Domestic Relations Court.

PHOTO BY DAVE GALEN

What started as an effort to showcase the quality beer that is brewed in the mid-Atlantic region is now a full-blown, three-day festival, featuring more than fifty craft and microbreweries from all across the country. Always the last weekend in June, the Old Dominion Beer Festival is far more than a place to taste new brews. The event—which now draws more than twenty thousand people over the weekend and sells enough beer to fill more than four hundred kegs—offers live music, activities for the children, local vendors with unique crafts and gifts, and food from area restaurants. The originator of the event, Old Dominion Brew Company, is the oldest craft brewery in Virginia, and produces twenty different beers, as well as root beer and ginger ale. A craft brewery produces between 15,001 and 100,000 barrels of beer annually; a microbrewery produces 15,000 or less. Beer brewing is an age-old art, as the technique is believed to have been developed by the earliest agrarian peoples in the Neolithic age. In preserving the quality of the craft, Old Dominion Brew Company adheres to the Old German Purity Laws that were written in Bavaria during the Middle Ages, using only pure water, barley and barley malt, and yeast to produce the beer.

PHOTO BY JEANETTE BURKLE

Destination … Not a Place, But a Perspective

Treat yourself to a new experience in recreation, relaxation, and rejuvenation

Featuring the amenities of a world-class resort located within reach of one of the nation's most exciting metropolitan areas, Lansdowne Resort offers its guests an out-of-the-ordinary vacation experience.

Opened in 1991 in Lansdowne, Virginia, as a Benchmark Hospitality International property, the resort quickly gained a reputation for top-notch meeting and conference services. In September 2004, management embarked on a $60 million renovation to expand its leisure offerings and transform Lansdowne into a full-service destination resort.

Located on over five hundred scenic and secluded acres, the AAA Four Diamond award-winning property is distinguished by luxury accommodations that include 305 guest rooms and nine suites. Stylish yet comfortable, these rooms and suites are designed to meet even the most discriminating traveler's needs, with readily available amenities like name-brand bath products, hair dryers, irons and ironing boards, oversized bath towels, coffeemakers, two-line phones with voice mail and modem line, and high-speed Internet.

Luxury also defines the treatments offered at Lansdowne's new twelve-thousand-square-foot Spa Minérale. Designed to pamper the body, mind, and spirit, the facility offers guests a host of massage and hydrotherapies, body wraps, facials, manicures and pedicures, and salon services. There's even a menu of treatments geared specifically for men. In addition, many of the spa's treatments and products feature indigenous botanicals and minerals. The nearby Goose Creek Rock

The Golf Club at Lansdowne is the area's premier private golf club, featuring forty-five holes of championship golf, exceptional practice facilities, and an architecturally stunning clubhouse, all combined with world-class resort amenities.

Quarry is harvested for inclusion in some of the spa's salts, scrubs, and muds, while Virginia's official tree and flower, the dogwood, is utilized to cleanse the skin, improve its clarity, and stimulate collagen production.

For many of the resort's guests, recreation is as important as relaxation. Rated among the nation's top golf resorts by publications like *Conde Nast Traveler* and *Golf* magazine, Lansdowne boasts eighteen-hole championship layouts by legendary designers Robert Trent Jones Jr. and Greg Norman. Norman has also designed a nine-hole course, adjacent to the eighteen-hole championship course, which offers more leisurely play perfect for beginners, juniors, and families. The private club also features a sixteen-acre practice facility and three large putting greens. The forty-five-thousand-square-foot clubhouse is perfect for relaxing before, after, or in between play, and is a popular spot for meetings and social gatherings.

Located next to the spa, the full-service health club provides guests with everything they need to maintain or jump-start a fitness routine. In addition to cardiovascular and weight training equipment, the club features tennis and racquetball courts, and fitness classes that cover everything from yoga and Pilates to spin and strength training. Aqua-based fitness classes are conducted at the indoor lap pool. On-staff personal trainers can provide quick advice on proper form or even personalized training plans.

Lansdowne serves as a perfect base from which to explore the region's myriad attractions.

continued on page 224

In addition to twelve treatment rooms, four relaxation lounges, and a complete image center, Spa Minerale features its own signature line of products, developed from indigenous botanicals and used in many of the treatments.

PHOTO BY SCOTT INDERMAUR

Interactive fountains and a waterslide, part of the resort's five-pool outdoor complex, make keeping cool fun for the whole family all summer long!

PHOTO BY SCOTT INDERMAUR

continued from page 223

A family-friendly resort, Lansdowne offers many amenities that appeal to younger guests. At the new aquatic complex, kids can enjoy waterslides and games at one pool while their parents relax in calming quiet at another. In-room Nintendo games and on-command movies provide the evening entertainment.

Since its renovation, Lansdowne has also become known for a variety of special events, many of them centered on music, wine, and fine dining. Guided by executive chef Jason Lage and renowned sommelier Mary Watson-DeLauder, the resort's Lansdowne Grille is one of the finest restaurants in the region, with a first-class wine program that has won a Wine Spectator Award of Excellence every year since 1995. Lage and Watson-DeLauder also conduct the resort's popular Food and Wine Camp Weekends, where guests have the opportunity to sample a variety of fine wines, all while enjoying two-night deluxe accommodations, a winery tour, a Friday evening reception and dinner, Saturday breakfast, a chef's table dinner, and a Sunday cooking class.

Food also plays a role in one of the resort's most successful charitable events. Held each year on or around Valentine's Day, the YMCA Loudoun County's annual

Lansdowne's Jazz on the Potomac summer concert series brings the community together for an evening of great food, drinks, and of course, live jazz, all under the stars on the resort's outdoor terrace.

PHOTO BY DAVE GALEN

All of the resort suites feature a spacious parlor, connecting bedrooms, and multiple balconies overlooking the Potomac River Valley and the resort's two golf courses.

PHOTO BY SCOTT INDERMAUR

Chocolates Galore invites local bakeries and restaurants to whip up their best chocolate-themed goodies, while guests sample the offerings along with fine champagnes. In 2006 the event attracted over eight hundred guests and raised nearly fifty thousand dollars to benefit the YMCA.

Lansdowne is also the originator of the Bobby Mitchell Hall of Fame Golf Tournament, one of the country's largest gatherings of Hall-of-Fame athletes at a charitable event. Held at the resort since it first opened, the tournament currently raises upwards of $1 million for the Leukemia & Lymphoma Society each year.

Located in the heart of Loudoun County, Lansdowne also serves as a perfect base from which to explore the region's myriad attractions. Everything from downtown Leesburg's antique shops to Washington, D.C.'s landmarks and museums are only a few minutes away by car. Secluded yet accessible, Lansdowne is the perfect spot to explore, relax, and ultimately rejuvenate. ✦

PHOTO BY DAVE GALEN

The annual Bobby Mitchell Hall of Fame Golf Classic, benefiting the Leukemia & Lymphoma Society, brings over fifty Pro Sports Hall of Famers to Lansdowne Resort each year.

PHOTO BY BRUCE R. FEELEY

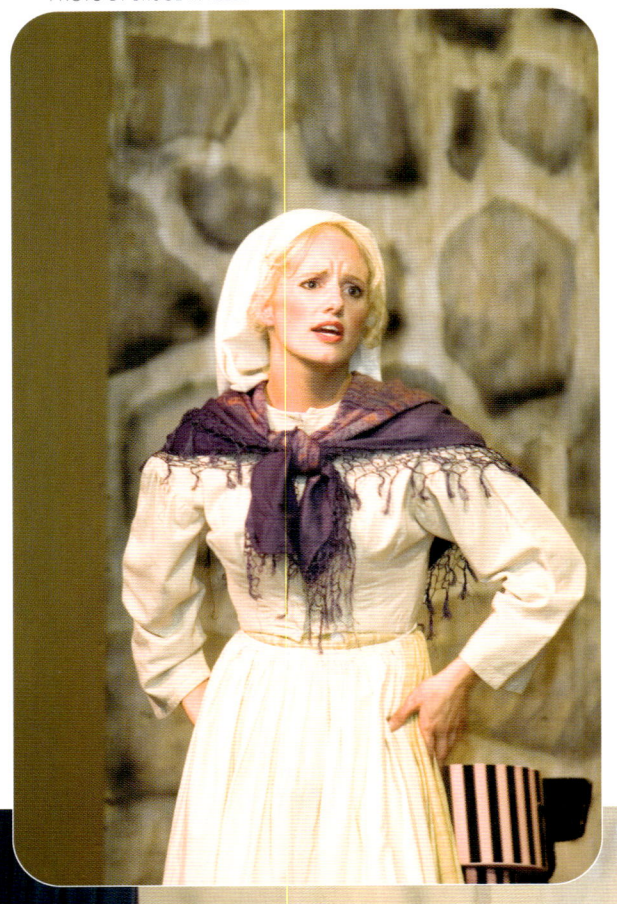

Community theater in Loudoun County is as magical as the story of Cinderella. Just as the young woman believed one day she'd find her prince, the budding actors and actresses in the community find their way to developing their craft through community organizations dedicated to theatre. "Loudoun has many nonprofit theatre companies that work well together. We also have great organizations that provide classes. The kids who grow up here and attend those classes go right into community theater fully trained," says Meredith Bean McMath, artistic director of the Aurora Studio Theatre, where productions like *Cinderella* come alive. Loudoun County's support of community theater is also evident in the new Franklin Park Performing Arts and Visual Center. Like Cinderella's pumpkin chariot, the new center sprung from two large barns, renovated to create an intimate theatre space, as well as areas for visual arts display and classes. The facility is county-owned, but a significant proportion of volunteer resources in the form of materials and time went into the reconstruction.

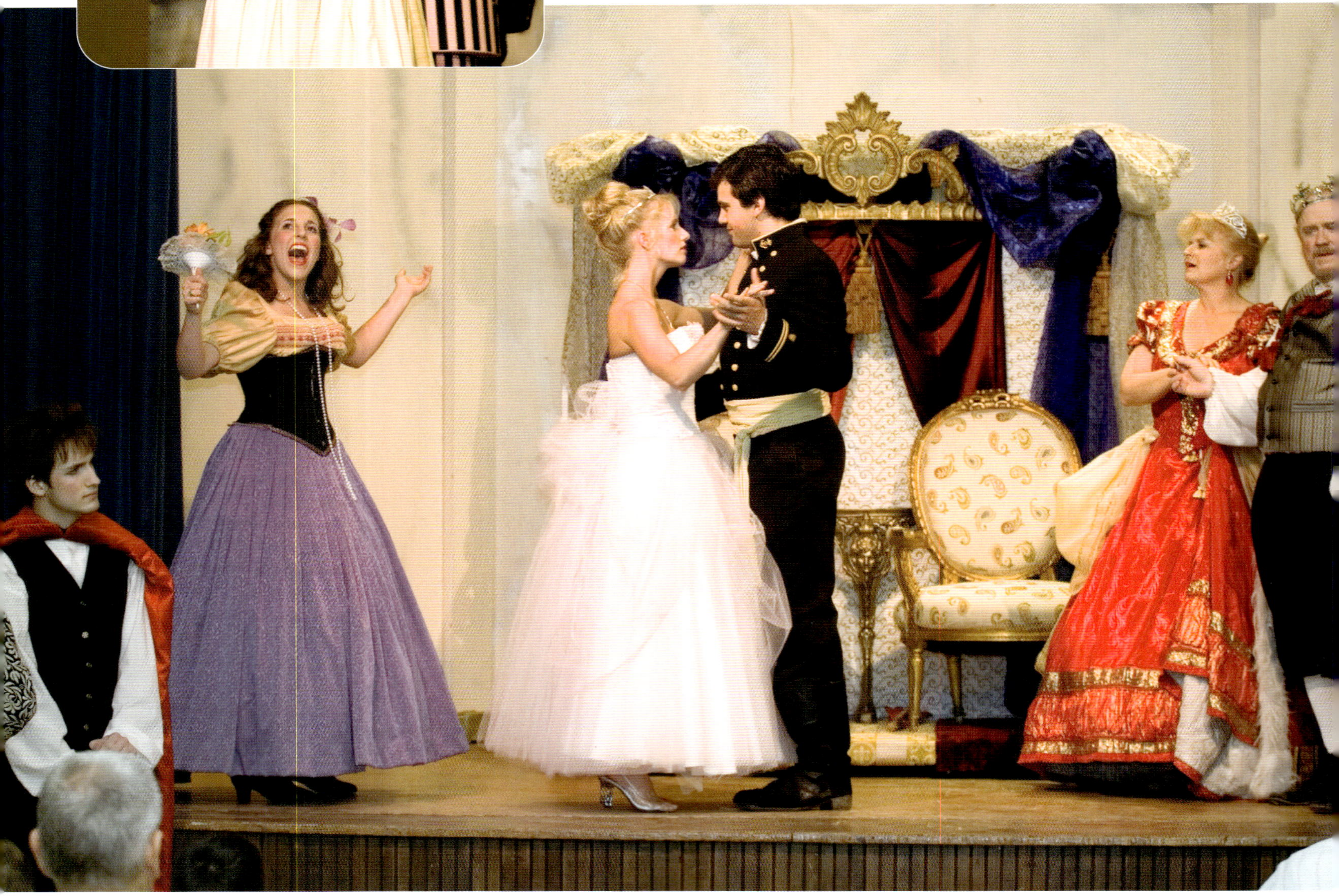

PHOTO BY BRUCE R. FEELEY

PHOTO BY ALAN S. WEINER

There's nothing like arriving in style, especially on prom night. Reston Limo has been catering to the needs of clients in the metro D.C. area since the 1980s. The fleet of more than one hundred vehicles is large enough to take care of any need, and the service is personal enough to make any event extraordinary. So the couple of the evening feels elegant, and parents can rest easy knowing that Reston is polished, prompt, and dependable.

If you drive along the John Mosby Highway, halfway between Alexandria and Winchester, you will find a fieldstone tavern built in 1728. The establishment came to be known as Chinn's Ordinary, named for Joseph Chinn, the builder. It was a popular stopping place for traveling colonists and remained so even after the land around it was sold to the newly chartered town of Middleburg. As the area's reputation for foxhunting, Thoroughbred breeding, and horse racing grew, Chinn's became the focal point for the community's social and economic activities. Over the years, however, the tavern and the inn fell on hard times. In 1937, a local citizen saved the building from the wrecking ball, did extensive remodeling, and renamed it the Red Fox Inn. Today, after more than two and a half centuries, the Red Fox Inn is still committed to providing good food, good wine, and efficient service. The Stray Fox makes up eight of the twenty-three rooms in the Red Fox Inn complex. There are seven cozy dining rooms, six of which have original working stone fireplaces and hand-hewn ceiling beams over thick stone and plaster walls.

PHOTO BY ALAN S. WEINER

The Mighty Midget Kitchen may be tiny, but its fan base is big. The Leesburg icon, built from a B29 bomber fuselage, is known for its specialty menu of mouth-watering barbecue, burgers, kielbasa, Black Angus beef hot dogs, and even alligator sausage. Owner Brian DeVaux took over "The Midget" in 2000. A competitive barbecuer, DeVaux fixes up slabs of his famous ribs on Fridays and Saturdays. Patrons come from all around the northern Virginia area for the award-winning barbecue and burgers, as well as for the backyard-style atmosphere that stirs up memories. "People bring their kids here because their fathers brought them here," DeVaux says. "But remember, we seat only outdoors, so we're open weather permitting."

PHOTO BY SCOTT INDERMAUR

"Tag, you're it." Or, in paintball, it's more like "Splat, you're out." The immensely popular sport of paintball appeals to competitors of all ages. A game similar to capture-the-flag, paintball combines the elements of precision, strategy, and fun. Participants ("ballers") use a compressed air gun to shoot at each other marble-sized capsules of a material that resembles paint. The game can be played indoors or outdoors, but in either setting, protective equipment is required for safety. Often, camouflage clothing is used for strategy. It's been said that the game of paintball began in Virginia in the mid-seventies, when two friends tried to re-create the excitement of a hunting trip. They used as their "weapon" a gun found in the agricultural industry for marking cattle, and they called their game Survival. Today the sport has millions of fans, including Jonathan Fazio, who heads out several weekends of each month to the paintball field. "It's what I do instead of golf," he says. "It's a great way to go out with a group of friends, let off steam, run around, and have fun." Fazio is a member of a team named Capital Offense—about eighteen East Coast friends who call this Loudoun County paintball field their home turf.

Spend the day testing the ripples of Goose Creek for smallmouth bass, and you'll remind yourself all over again why fly-fishing is as much an art as a science. A small waterfall created by the remnants of an old mill and the shadows of Coton Bridge that crosses the creek create an excellent habitat for fishing and an excellent occasion for anglers to hone their finesse. Goose Creek and the Potomac River are two waterways accessible from Loudoun County that support a variety of fish species, including smallmouth and largemouth bass, tiger muskie, crappie, channel catfish, redbreast sunfish, walleye, and carp.

PHOTO BY ALAN S. WEINER

Featured
COMPANIES

ACCESS REALTY
9 North King Street
Leesburg, Virginia 20176
703.777.8737

Real Estate—Residential
Access Realty, founded by Kathy Samson and Steve Harrison in 2001, specializes in residential, commercial, and historic real estate, as well as land sales and other real estate transactions. The company's nearly thirty real estate agents, as well as Samson and Harrison, hold licenses to practice real estate in Virginia, Maryland, and Florida.

PAGES 158–159

AMERICAN HOME MORTGAGE
44365 Premier Plaza
Suite 200
Ashburn, Virginia 20147
571.223.0189
866.324.2900
www.americanhm.com/maryam.mcdaniel

Financial Institution—Mortgage Company
American Home Mortgage in Loudoun County is a branch of American Home Mortgage nationwide. *Fortune* magazine ranks AHM as the second-fastest-growing company in America. The branch offers residential mortgage loan products for first-time, move-up, and investment home buyers.

PAGES 70–71

AOL LLC
22000 AOL Way
Dulles, Virginia 20166
www.corp.aol.com

Internet Service Provider
With its headquarters in Dulles, Virginia, online services pioneer AOL operates a leading network of Web brands in addition to the largest Internet subscription service in the United States.

PAGES 142–145

BRIDGMAN COMMUNICATIONS
45064 Underwood Lane, Suite 100
Dulles, Virginia 20166-9513
703.471.4700
www.bridgmancom.com

Telecommunications
Located in Dulles since 1983, this professional interconnect telephone organization specializes in providing businesses and organizations with the most effective and efficient solutions for their telecommunications needs.

PAGES 148–149

**DULLES AREA ASSOCIATION
OF REALTORS®, INC.**
803 Sycolin Road, Suite 222
Leesburg, Virginia 20175
45005 Aviation Drive, Suite 201
Dulles, Virginia 20166
703.777.2468
888.475.2468
www.dullesarea.com

Real Estate—Association
Since 1962, DAAR has contributed to the development of ethical, knowledgeable, and effective real estate professionals serving Loudoun County as well as the state of Virginia and the D.C. area.

PAGES 32–34

DUNLAP, GRUBB & WEAVER
199 Liberty Street SW
Leesburg, Virginia 20175
703.777.7319
www.dglegal.com

Law Firm
Dunlap, Grubb & Weaver is a law firm practicing in intellectual property, corporate and business law, and real estate. With offices in Leesburg and the metropolitan Washington area, and licensed to practice in eleven states, Dunlap, Grubb & Weaver is uniquely positioned to serve clients in local, national, and global markets.

PAGES 110–111

F & M TITLE & ESCROW
44365 Premier Plaza, Suite 210
Ashburn, Virginia 20147
571.223.2530
www.fmtitle.net

Financial Institution—Title and Escrow Company
F & M Title & Escrow deals mostly with professional-based customers such as Realtors and mortgage bankers. Their bottom line is to assure all customers of a complete, legally binding process that gives them the insurance they need at fair and reasonable prices.

PAGE 72

THOMAS BALCH LIBRARY
208 West Market Street
Leesburg, Virginia 20176
703.737.7195
www.leesburgva.gov/services/library
www.balchfriends.com

Library
Thomas Balch Library specializes in the history and genealogy of Leesburg, Loudoun County, and Virginia. In addition to research collections, the town-operated library offers special programs, events, and classes.

PAGES 38–39

GEORGE MASON UNIVERSITY
4400 University Drive
Fairfax, Virginia 22030
703.993.1000
www.gmu.edu

School—University
One of the most respected universities in the nation, George Mason University is known for its diverse student body and exceptional graduate and undergraduate programs in a wide range of disciplines.

PAGES 54–56

GEORGE WASHINGTON UNIVERSITY VIRGINIA CAMPUS, THE
Research Building 1 (original building)
20101 Academic Way
Ashburn, Virginia 20147
Administration Building
44983 Knoll Square
Ashburn, Virginia 20147
703.726.8200
http://gwvirginia.gwu.edu

School—University
The George Washington University Virginia Campus, created to meet the growing demands of the area's technology and telecommunications sectors, offers more than twenty graduate certificate and degree programs in education, business, and engineering; an undergraduate degree in pharmacogenomics; and undergraduate and graduate certificates in fields ranging from aviation to landscaping. The campus houses more than fifteen research centers, laboratories, and institutes.

PAGES 92–93

GREENVEST L.C.
8614 Westwood Center Drive
Suite 900
Vienna, Virginia 22182
703.422.8992
www.thevillagesatdullessouth.com

Real Estate—Developer
Greenvest is a residential builder of planned communities. Their concept for The Villages at Dulles South is to bring world-class amenities to Loudoun County while providing a place for generations of Loudoun's future families to live, work, and grow. These four distinct villages are a new way of creating lifetime communities for tomorrow.

PAGES 136–137

HCA NORTHERN VIRGINIA
1850 Town Center Parkway
Reston, Virginia 20190
703.858.3465
www.hcahealthcare.com

Hospital—Medical Center
HCA Virginia is a comprehensive health-care network that operates eleven medical facilities throughout the state. In northern Virginia, the organization provides extensive medical services at Reston Hospital Center, Northern Virginia Community Hospital, Reston Surgery Center, Fairfax Surgical Center, and Dominion Hospital, the region's only mental health hospital. In 2010, HCA Virginia will open two new full-service hospitals: Broadlands Regional Medical Center and Spotsylvania Regional Medical Center. HCA Virginia is part of HCA Hospitals, the nation's largest hospital network.

PAGES 96–99

HOLIDAY INN AT HISTORIC CARRODOC HALL
1500 East Market Street
Leesburg, Virginia 20176
703.771.9200
www.holiday-inn.com/leesburg.va

Hotel
Conveniently located in historic Leesburg, just fourteen miles from Dulles International Airport, the Holiday Inn at Historic Carrodoc Hall features 126 guest rooms and ample meeting space, making it an ideal location for business and pleasure.

PAGES 188–190

HOWARD HUGHES MEDICAL INSTITUTE
19700 Helix Drive
Ashburn, Virginia 20147
571.209.4000
www.hhmi.org

School—Medical Institute
The Janelia Farm Research Campus is Howard Hughes Medical Institute's first freestanding campus. The $500 million complex provides a unique setting in which small research groups can explore fundamental biomedical questions in a highly collaborative, interdisciplinary culture.

PAGES 64–67

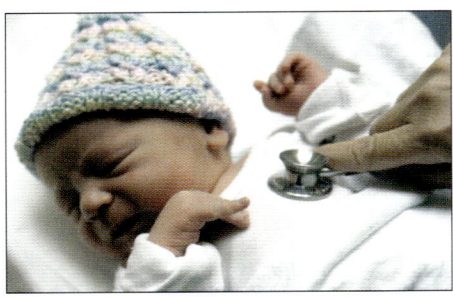

INOVA LOUDOUN HOSPITAL
44045 Riverside Parkway
Leesburg, Virginia 20176
703.858.6000
www.inova.org

Hospital—Medical Center
The residents of Loudoun County have been provided with quality care by Inova Loudoun Hospital since 1912. As a not-for-profit health-care institution, the hospital has no stockholders to satisfy, only the citizens who count on it to provide for their needs.

PAGES 22–25

LADIES BOARD OF INOVA LOUDOUN HOSPITAL, THE
44045 Riverside Parkway
Leesburg, Virginia 20176
703.771.2985
www.ladiesboard.org

Non-Profit Auxiliary Organization
Established with the founding of Loudoun Hospital in 1912, this nonprofit volunteer organization is devoted to promoting goodwill between the hospital and the community, while raising funds for its patients and services and providing scholarships to qualifying nursing students.

PAGES 14–15

LANSDOWNE RESORT
44050 Woodbridge Parkway
Lansdowne, Virginia 20176
703.729.8400
www.lansdowneresort.com

Hotel—Resort
As a world-class vacation and event destination, Lansdowne Resort offers guests opportunities for relaxation and rejuvenation among the scenic rural splendor of northern Virginia. Only minutes away from area attractions that include Washington, D.C., Lansdowne is also a perfect spot from which to explore the region.

PAGES 222–225

LOUDOUN COUNTY
1 Harrison Street SE
MSC #63
Leesburg, Virginia 20175
703.777.0426
biz.loudoun.gov

Government—County

By providing top-notch services and establishing beneficial public/private partnerships, Loudoun County provides residents of one of the fastest-growing regions in the nation with expanding economic opportunity and an unsurpassed quality of life.

PAGES 48–51

LOUDOUN COUNTY CHAMBER OF COMMERCE
101 Blue Seal Drive, Suite 100
Leesburg, Virginia 20175
703.777.2176
www.loudounchamber.org

Chamber of Commerce

In the last three decades, the population of Loudoun County has nearly quadrupled. The present-day Loudoun County Chamber of Commerce is a premier business organization in one of the nation's fastest-growing and most economically robust counties in the nation. Currently it serves more than thirteen hundred members, ranging from small businesses, sole proprietorships, and home-based businesses to major national and international firms.

PAGES 28–29

LOUDOUN MEDICAL GROUP
222 Catoctin Circle SE
Suite 200
Leesburg, Virginia 20175
703.737.6010
www.lmgdoctors.com

Physician Group

Serving over eight hundred thousand patients a year, this physician-directed medical group is one of the largest of its kind in Virginia. As a leading area employer, it also provides for the well-being of its 460-person staff and, via its charitable foundation, lends a helping hand to communities in need.

PAGES 80–83

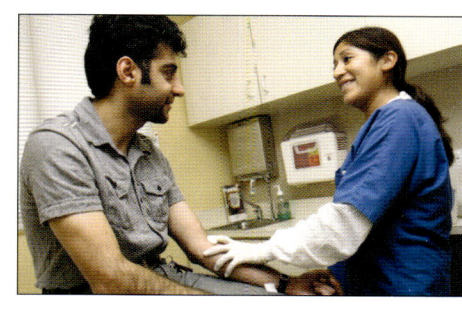

M. C. DEAN
22461 Shaw Road
Dulles, Virginia 20166
703.471.8041
800.762.3326
www.mcdean.com

Manufacturing

"Building intelligence" is the goal of this leading designer, builder, and integrator of complex electrical, telecommunications, and electronic systems. As a result, businesses, institutions, and governments on five continents can provide their services more safely, efficiently, and effectively.

PAGES 152–154

MERCANTILE POTOMAC BANK
6901 Rockledge Drive, Suite 510
Bethesda, Maryland 20817
301.963.7607
www.mercantilepotomacbank.com

Financial Institution—Bank

As a full-service community bank, Mercantile Potomac Bank offers a complete range of checking, savings, loan, and cash management options for individuals and businesses alike. In addition, through its Mercantile Investment & Wealth Management division, the bank offers a comprehensive array of products designed to ensure a secure future.

PAGES 122–124

METROPOLITAN WASHINGTON AIRPORTS AUTHORITY
1 Aviation Circle
Washington, DC 20001
703.417.8370
www.mwaa.com

Airport

The Metropolitan Washington Airports Authority operates a two-airport system that provides domestic and international air service for the mid-Atlantic region. It is an independent body created by the Commonwealth of Virginia and the District of Columbia, approved by Congress to operate and maintain Ronald Reagan Washington National Airport and Washington Dulles International Airport.

PAGES 128–129

MILES LEHANE COMPANIES, THE
205 North King Street
Leesburg, Virginia 20176
703.777.3370
www.mileslehane.com

Consultants
The Miles LeHane Companies focuses its services for companies and individuals on career management issues including career transition, executive coaching, training and development, and human resources consulting. It is headquartered in the Glenfiddich House, an 1840s mansion, that serves as a tranquil in-residence retreat for executives progressing into a new stage in their careers.

PAGE 132

MOORE CADILLAC HUMMER
25440 Pleasant Valley Road
Chantilly, Virginia 20152
703.674.5900
www.moorecadillac.com

Automobile Dealer
As the premier Cadillac Hummer dealership in the region, Moore Cadillac Hummer expanded its presence in high-end automobile sales in 2005, with the addition of its new Chantilly location.

PAGES 216–218

N.E.W. CUSTOMER SERVICE COMPANIES, INC.
22894 Pacific Boulevard
Sterling, Virginia 20166
703.788.5428
www.newcorp.com

Warranty Company
NEW is the nation's leading provider of extended service contracts and buyer protection programs for consumer products. In an average year, *NEW* call centers nationwide handle nearly 11 million telephone, email, and fax interactions. The company has been recognized for the second consecutive year by J.D. Power and Associates for providing outstanding customer service.

PAGES 116–119

NOTRE DAME ACADEMY
35321 Notre Dame Lane
Middleburg, Virginia 20117
540.687.5581
www.notredameva.org

School—Private College Preparatory
Notre Dame Academy is an independent, Catholic coeducational college preparatory high school located in a pastoral Virginia setting approximately forty miles west of Washington, D.C. The diverse population of approximately three hundred students enjoys rigorous academics, strong athletic programs, multidimensional extracurricular activities, and participation in community service.

PAGES 76–77

NOVA MEDICAL GROUP & URGENT CARE CENTER, INC.
The Medical Spa at Nova
21785 Filigree Court, Suite 100
Ashburn, Virginia 20147
703.554.1100
www.novamedgroup.com
www.novaurgentcare.com
www.novamedspa.com

Medical Group—Health Spa
Nova Medical Group & Urgent Care Center, Inc. offers Loudoun County patients primary, acute, and alternative care under one roof. Nova integrates traditional Western medicine with complementary medicine, including naturopathic and Oriental medicine, acupuncture, and other therapies. The practice boasts four locations in Sterling, Leesburg, Warrenton, and Ashburn. In January 2005, Nova added the Medical Spa at Nova to the Ashburn location.

PAGES 42–45

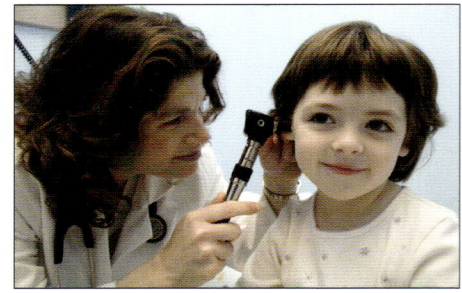

OLD DOMINION UNIVERSITY, NORTHERN VIRGINIA CENTER
21335 Signal Hill Plaza, Suite 300
Sterling, Virginia 20164
703.948.2750
www.odu.edu/nvc

School—University
From its Northern Virginia Center, Old Dominion University brings Loudoun County access to undergraduate and graduate degrees via distance learning technologies. Offering a wide range of formats and schedules, combined with quality on-site and online student services, ODU makes it convenient for working professionals to pursue their academic goals in Loudoun County.

PAGE 18

RASPBERRY FALLS GOLF & HUNT CLUB
41601 Raspberry Drive
Leesburg, Virginia 20176
703.589.1042

Golf Club
Raspberry Falls Golf & Hunt Club is Virginia's only Gary Player Signature Design Scottish links–style golf course. The public course is a 7,191-yard, par-72 layout using the natural attributes of land that was once one of the most fertile plantations in the state.

PAGES 168–169

RE/MAX LEADERS, SHERRY WILSON & CO.
1021 East Main Street
Purcellville, Virginia 20132
540.338.6300
800.303.0115
www.sherrywilson.com
sherryw@sherrywilson.com

Real Estate—Residential
A bona fide leader in the real estate industry, RE/MAX Leaders Sherry Wilson & Co. has been the number-one RE/MAX Agent/Team in Virginia and the Central Atlantic Region since 1999, as well as the number-two, -three, or -four RE/MAX Agent/Team in the United States and Across the World every year since 2000. The team, which specializes in Loudoun County and surrounding northern Virginia areas, consists of more than twenty full-time members, including Wilson, several real estate agents, and a dedicated administrative staff.

PAGES 86–88

REHAU
1501 Edwards Ferry Road, NE
Leesburg, Virginia 20176
703.777.5255
www.rehau.com

Manufacturing
REHAU is a worldwide leader in the manufacture of polymer-based systems for construction, automotive, and industry.

PAGE 106

RESTON LIMOUSINE
45685 Elmwood Court
Dulles, Virginia 20166
703.478.0500
www.restonlimo.com

Limousine Service
Reston Limousine is the largest, fully licensed limo company providing service round the clock in Virginia, Washington, D.C., and Maryland. Currently it has 135 vehicles serving government agencies, universities, embassies, airports, and hospitals in the tri-state area. Reston is the only transportation company ever to receive an award from the U.S. government.

PAGES 202–203

RITZ-CARLTON GOLF CLUB, CREIGHTON FARMS, THE
22616 James Monroe Highway
Aldie, Virginia 20105
877.300.3338
www.creightonfarms.com

Country Club Community
The Ritz-Carlton Golf Club, Creighton Farms is a spectacular residential country club community combining the unique qualities of developers Juno Properties, LLC, The Ritz-Carlton, and Nicklaus Design. Residents and nonresident members enjoy The Ritz-Carlton standard of excellence within the gracious lifestyle of a country club community.

PAGES 208–211

SEVERN MORTGAGE
35 North Braddock Street
Winchester, Virginia 22601
540.678.4141

521C East Market Street
Leesburg, Virginia 20176
703.779.2225
www.SevernMortgage.com

Financial Institution—Mortgage Company
Since 1998, this locally owned and operated mortgage banking company has helped clients throughout Loudoun County realize their dream of home ownership. From start to finish, the company's professionals provide expert guidance and advice, resulting in the right loan at the best possible price.

PAGES 60–61

THE TOWN OF LEESBURG

25 West Market Street
Leesburg, Virginia 20178
703.771.2734
www.leesburgva.gov

Government—City

Founded in 1756, the Town of Leesburg is the county seat for Loudoun County, Virginia. Home to more than thirty thousand residents and covering twelve square miles, Leesburg is distinguished by its historical charm, a spirit of friendliness and hospitality, and a prospering business environment.

PAGES 194–197

THOMPSON HOSPITALITY CORPORATION

505 Huntmar Park Drive, Suite 350
Herndon, Virginia 20170

Ashburn Car Wash
43324 Junction Plaza
Ashburn, Virginia 20147
www.ashburncarwash.com

Food Service and Car Wash

Ashburn Car Wash is owned and operated by Thompson Hospitality Corporation, one of the nation's largest minority-owned businesses. Ashburn Car Wash is open seven days a week, from 8 a.m. until 7 p.m.

PAGE 182

UNITED AIRLINES

Dulles International Airport
44835 Package Court
Equipment Maintenance Building
Dulles, Virginia 20166
800.864.8331
www.united.com

Airline

United Airlines has served Loudoun County and the Washington, D.C., community for over sixty years. Nationwide, it operates more than thirty-seven hundred flights a day to more than 210 domestic and international destinations. United also employs five thousand people locally, making it Loudoun County's fourth-largest employer.

PAGES 174–177

PHOTO BY BRUCE R. FEELEY

Two young spectators enjoy the activities of the Loudoun County Hunt Club.

EDITORIAL TEAM

Kimberly Fox DeMeza, *Writer, Roswell, Georgia.* Combining business insight with creative flair, DeMeza writes to engage the audience as well as communicate the nuances of the subject matter. While officially beginning her career in public relations in 1980 with a degree in journalism, and following in 1990 with a master's in health management, writing has always been central to her professional experience. From speechwriting to corporate brochures to business magazine feature writing, DeMeza enjoys the process of crafting the message. Delving into the topic is simply one of the benefits, as she believes every writing opportunity is an opportunity to continue to learn.

Rena Distasio, *Writer, Tijeras, New Mexico.* Freelance writer Rena Distasio contributes articles and reviews on a variety of subjects to regional and national publications. In her spare time she and her husband and three dogs enjoy the great outdoors from their home in the mountains east of Albuquerque.

Grace Hawthorne, *Writer, Atlanta, Georgia.* Starting as a reporter, she has written everything from advertising for septic tanks to the libretto for an opera. While in New York, she worked for Time-Life Books and wrote for Sesame Street. As a performer, she has appeared at the Carter Presidential Center, Callanwolde Fine Arts Center, and at various corporate functions. Her latest project is a two-woman show called Pushy Broads and Proper Southern Ladies.

Amy Meadows, *Writer, Canton, Georgia.* Meadows is an accomplished feature writer who has been published in a wide variety of local, regional, and national consumer and trade publications since launching her freelance writing career in 2000. She also specializes in producing corporate marketing literature for companies large and small and holds a masters of arts degree in professional writing from Kennesaw State University.

Regina Roths, *Writer, Andover, Kansas.* Roths has written extensively about business since launching her journalism career in the early 1990s. Her prose can be found in corporate coffee-table books nationwide as well as on regionally produced Web sites, and in print and online magazines, newspapers, and publications. Her love of industry, history, and research gives her a keen insight into writing and communicating a message.

Jeanette Galie Burkle, *Photographer, Leesburg, Virginia.* The owner of Galie Photography, a studio that specializes in weddings and environmental portraits of families, Jeanette has one main attraction to the medium of photography—emotional resonance. Jeanette is able to transfer this same passion to other areas of photography as well, an ability demonstrated by her nationally and locally published photographs in magazines ranging from *County Sampler's County Business* to *Loudoun Magazine* and *Elan.* Jeanette has exhibited her fine art photography at local galleries and art shows in Northern Virginia. View more of Jeanette's work at www.galiephotography.com.

Thomas S. England, *Photographer, Decatur, Georgia.* England grew up internationally, graduated from Northwestern University, and began photography as a newspaper photographer in the Chicago area. He began freelancing for *People* magazine in 1974. Since then he has taken assignments from national magazines and corporations, specializing in photographing people on location. He lives in Decatur, Georgia, with Nancy Foster, a home renovator, and their dog Chessey. More of his photographs may be viewed online at www.englandphoto.com.

Bruce R. Feeley, *Photographer, Raleigh, North Carolina.* Feeley has worked for various news agencies over the past twenty-five years in the northeast and southeast. After leaving New York he worked as a staff photographer at Duke University for seven years. He is a regular contributor to *The New York Times,* and his work from the American Dance Festival, in Durham, North Carolina, is in the Local Legacies permanent collection at The Smithsonian in Washington, D.C. His work is primarily editorial and has appeared in *U.S. News & World Report, Sports Illustrated, USA Today,* and numerous foreign publications. His proudest accomplishment is being a dad to his five-year-old son, Ian James Feeley.

Dave Galen, *Photographer, Leesburg, Virginia,* David Galen began his business in 1991 as the result of a lifelong hobby. Galen Photography evolved from photographing special events for trade associations to becoming the Galen Group, Inc., a commercial imaging service. Mr. Galen specializes in advertising, architecture and interiors, corporate, and industrial photography. His architectural and interior photographs have won awards repeatedly for his clients from the Associated Builders and Contractors, the National Commercial Builders Council, and the Northern Virginia Building Industry Association. His work is featured in *Loudoun County—Blending Tradition with Innovation, Loudoun Magazine,* and advertising published by several government and corporate clients throughout the metropolitan Washington, D.C., area.

Scott Indermaur, *Photographer, Lawrence, Kansas.* Indermaur received a degree in journalism with an emphasis on photography at Northern Arizona University. Scott then moved to Kansas in 1992 to start his independent career, combining photography with his enthusiasm and knowledge of computers and programming. Having enjoyed the fast-paced atmosphere of journalistic photography, he decided to turn his focus to environmental portraiture for corporate annual reports, editorial magazines, and advertising. Scott lives with his wife, children, dogs, and a cat in Lawrence, Kansas, where he is also a fine food and wine enthusiast. You can find more information about Scott at www.siphotography.com.

Alan S. Weiner, *Photographer, Portland, Oregon.* Weiner travels extensively both in the United States and abroad. Over the last twenty-three years his work has appeared regularly in *The New York Times.* In addition, his pictures have been published in *USA Today* and in *Time, Newsweek, Life,* and *People* magazines. He has shot corporate work for IBM, Pepsi, UPS, and other companies large and small. He is also the cofounder of The Wedding Bureau (www.weddingbureau.com). Alan has worked in every region of the country for Riverbend Books. His strengths are in photojournalism.

ABOUT THE PUBLISHER

Loudoun County — A Photographic Portrait was published by Bookhouse Group, Inc., under its imprint of Riverbend Books. What many people don't realize is that in addition to picture books on American communities, we also develop and publish institutional histories, commemorative books of all types, contemporary books, and others for clients across the country.

Bookhouse has developed various types of books for prep schools from Utah to Florida, colleges and universities, country clubs, a phone company in Vermont, a church in Atlanta, hospitals, banks, and many other entities. We've also published a catalog for an art collection for a gallery in Texas, a picture book for a worldwide Christian ministry, and a book on a priceless collection of art and antiques for the Atlanta History Center.

These beautiful and treasured tabletop books are developed by our staff as turnkey projects, thus making life easier for the client. If your company has an interest in our publishing services, do not hesitate to contact us.

Founded in 1989, Bookhouse Group is headquartered in a renovated 1920s tobacco warehouse in downtown Atlanta. If you're ever in town, we'd be delighted if you looked us up. Thank you for making possible the publication of *Loudoun County — A Photographic Portrait*.

Banks ✦ Prep Schools ✦ Hospitals ✦ Insurance Companies ✦ Art Galleries ✦ Museums ✦ Utilities
✦ Country Clubs ✦ Colleges ✦ Churches ✦ Military Academies ✦ Associations

BOOKHOUSE
GROUP, INC.